INFORMATION SYSTEMS USING DSS SOFTWARE

Dr. Ronald D. Schwartz
Wilkes University

Dale P. Bonar

Gregory D. Kosicki

boyd & fraser publishing company

ITP   An International Thomson Publishing Company

Danvers • Albany • Bonn • Boston • Cincinnati • Detroit • London • Madrid • Melbourne
Mexico City • New York • Paris • San Francisco • Singapore • Tokyo • Toronto • Washington

Publishing Process Director: Carol Crowell
Acquisitions Editor: Rita Ferrandino
Production Editor: Jean Bermingham
Composition: Monotype Composition Co., Inc.
Interior Design: Sandy Weinstein/Tin Box Studio
Cover Design: Sandy Weinstein/Tin Box Studio
Manufacturing Coordinator: Carol Chase
Marketing Director: William Lisowski

Printed in the United States of America

For more information, contact boyd & fraser publishing company:

boyd & fraser publishing company
One Corporate Place • Ferncroft Village
Danvers, Massachusetts 01923, USA

International Thomson Editores
Campose Eliseos 385, Piso 7
Col. Polanco
11560 Mexico D.F. Mexico

International Thomson Publishing Europe
Berkshire House 168-173
High Holborn
London, WC1V 7AA, England

International Thomson Publishing GmbH
Konigswinterer Strasse 418
53227 Bonn, Germany

Thomas Nelson Australia
102 Dodds Street
South Melbourne 3205
Victoria, Australia

International Thomson Publishing Asia
221 Henderson Road
#05-10 Henderson Building
Singapore 0315

Nelson Canada
1120 Birchmount Road
Scarborough, Ontario
Canada M1K 5G4

International Thomson Publishing Japan
Hirakawacho Kyowa Building, 3F
2-2-1 Hirakawacho
Chiyoda-ku, Tokyo 102, Japan

1 2 3 4 5 6 7 8 9 10 PN 9 8 7 6 5

ISBN: 0-7895-0120-1

Dedication

to Sheldon Berns,

a person of the utmost integrity and professionalism

CONTENTS

PREFACE

Information Systems Using DDS Software can be used to support three types of courses: (1) required introductory MIS/CIS courses; (2) courses in Decision Theory/Computer Problem Solving; and (3) elective courses in Decision Support Systems (DSS). This book assumes that the student has completed a recent course in computer literacy and has attained operational proficiency using word processing, spreadsheet analysis, and database management software.

METHODOLOGY

The authors utilize a computer problem-solving approach as the primary focus of the book. Through the use of DSS software packages, students become active participants in the learning environment. This pragmatic approach enables students to expand and fine-tune their analytical skills.

ORGANIZATION

This text is comprised of twelve modules covering the topics of problem solving, knowledge-based systems, and programming languages. Each module has a stated objective, example problems, and student exercises.

SOFTWARE

The software used in the DSS modules is oriented to IBM and IBM-compatible personal computers. The software packages include the following:

Word Processing:	WordPerfect
Spreadsheet Analysis:	Lotus 1-2-3
Statistical Analysis:	Minitab
Markov Analysis:	Computer Models for Management Science (CMMS)
Linear Programming:	Computer Models for Management Science (CMMS)
Expert Systems:	VP-Expert
Database Management Systems:	dBASE IV
BASIC Programming:	QuickBASIC
PASCAL Programming:	Dr. PASCAL
FORTRAN Programming:	Microsoft FORTRAN
COBOL Programming:	Microsoft COBOL
SQL Programming:	dBASE IV

It should be noted that student exercises can be completed using any other comparable software package. For example, Microsoft Word could be used in place of WordPerfect, or Microsoft Excel could be used instead of Lotus 1-2-3. Students and professors have complete flexibility in deciding which software packages are to be used in problem solving.

A NOTE TO THE INSTRUCTOR

Students are assumed to have the fundamental productivity skills in word processing, spreadsheet analysis, and database management. All modules reinforce basic productivity skills and gradually expand students' problem-solving capabilities.

We have written this book to facilitate flexibility for the instructor. We recognize that there may be several topics or modules that some instructors would rather de-emphasize or even omit. The text is set up so that instructors are free to select the modules which they desire to emphasize. Ample exercises are provided for individual and/or group problem-solving assignments.

ACKNOWLEDGMENTS

The origin of this textbook can be traced back to Dr. Schwartz's participation in the 1987 Advanced Management Information Systems Development Institute sponsored by AACSB (American Assembly of Collegiate Schools of Business) and directed by Dr. Milton Jenkins. The Institute provided Dr. Schwartz with a foundation in information systems curriculum development. From this foundation, the pedagogy applied in this textbook evolved.

These materials have been classroom tested at both Wayne State and Wilkes Universities. Comments and suggestions received from students enrolled in MIS/CIS courses have been incorporated into the text.

I am extremely grateful to Ms. Charlene Frail for her diligent effort in word processing a very demanding manuscript, and to Ms. Rebecca Kennedy for her valuable editing and encouragement while I completed the manuscript. Also, special thanks to all of the people at boyd & fraser publishing company who contributed to the development and production of the text. In particular, Jean Bermingham must be thanked for her diligent production efforts, and Tony Palermino for his copyediting skills. A final note of gratitude is extended to Sandy Weinstein—a wonderfully talented graphic artist responsible for the outstanding interior design and attractive cover design of this text.

Ronald Schwartz

INTRODUCTION

One of the primary objectives of a course in Information Systems (IS) is to develop and enhance problem-solving skills for decision makers. This text introduces these skills by using Decision Support Systems (DSS) packages for problem solving. In the past, IS classes have been successful in providing solutions to structured types of problems, that is, problems having rules for decision making that are well defined. Two examples of structured problems are (a) whether or not credit should be extended to a customer, or (b) when should items be reordered from inventory. IS courses have been less successful, however, providing students with a repertoire of problem-solving tools for solving semistructured or unstructured problems. For these two types of problems, there is no set of well-defined, formalized rules for problem solving.

Firms have been lagging in their efforts to provide their employees with the fundamental IS tools beyond basic productivity tools such as Lotus 1-2-3, dBase IV, and WordPerfect. As a consequence, DSS tools are minimally utilized in the corporate environment. These organizations must realize the importance and full capabilities of advanced computer packages such as Minitab, Computer Models for Management Science (CMMS), and VP-Expert systems. A second tier of problem solving capability beyond the initial endeavors of the productivity skills is needed and must be imparted to employees within these organizations. This manuscript is an attempt to address this deficiency.

METHODOLOGY

The traditional pedagogy in a typical MIS course is a lecture/case approach where the student is essentially a passive learner in a minimally stimulating environment.

However, using DSS packages, a student can become a truly active participant in a learning environment that is highly motivational and emphasizes the important managerial skills of problem solving and critical thinking.

This text provides actual business applications for computer problem solving. It assumes students have the fundamental skills to operate these DSS packages. Students are expected to have a basic comprehension of WordPerfect, Lotus 1-2-3, Minitab, Computer Models for Management Science, and VP-Expert.

CONTENT

This text presents twelve modules covering problem solving, knowledge-based systems, and programming languages. Each module contains problem-solving examples and student exercises and is organized as follows:

- Objective
- Example Problems
- Exercises

A Decision Support System (DSS) is an integrated set of computer tools that allow a decision maker to interact with computers to create information useful in problem-solving and decision making.

COMPONENTS OF A DSS

The DSS software components are illustrated in the following table. The major components of DSS are: problem solving, knowledge-based systems, and programming languages.

The components of a DSS take the following format.

Problem Solving	Knowledge Base	Programming Languages
1. WordPerfect	1. VP-Expert	1. BASIC
2. Lotus 1-2-3	2. dBase IV	2. PASCAL
3. Minitab		3. FORTRAN
4. Markov Analysis		4. COBOL
5. Linear Programming		5. SQL

The problem-solving component is the backbone of the Decision Support System. It provides a multitude of capabilities including mathematical modeling, statistical analysis, spreadsheet analysis, analytical graphics, computation of Markov probabilities, and linear programming.

The knowledge-based component is comprised of both an expert system as well as a dBase IV programming module. It utilizes a knowledge-based domain for storing the knowledge of a human expert. The knowledge base interacts with an inference engine which logically determines which steps to undertake in order to solve the problem.

DSS programming languages are comprised of procedural and non-procedural languages. A procedural language requires the user to write logical steps or procedural instructions to solve a given problem. Typical procedural languages include BASIC, FORTRAN, COBOL, and PASCAL. A non-procedural language merely requires that the user supply an executable command. The logic is already built into the language. Therefore the information requested is promptly displayed after the command is executed. SQL is an example of a non-procedural language.

FUNCTIONS OF A DSS

A comprehensive and efficient DSS should provide the user with the following problem-solving techniques:

- Procedural and non-procedural programming languages
- Model building utilizing linear and multiple linear regression

- What-if analysis using spreadsheets to determine the impact of changes within a financial analysis
- Descriptive and inferential statistical analysis
- Analytical graphics to visually illustrate and interpret the context of selected variables

PART I

PROBLEM-SOLVING MODULES

The Problem-Solving Modules are designed to enhance the critical thinking skills students will need to arrive at a viable solution to a given problem. The deliberate use of practical, true-to-life exercises serves to reinforce the decision-making process by offering students examples of problems typically encountered by many corporations in today's complex business world.

■

The software tools used in this section include WordPerfect, Lotus 1-2-3, Minitab, and CMMS. These tools offer the student the opportunity to analyze problems and arrive at an appropriate solution. It is assumed that the student is familiar with the fundamentals of each DSS tool.

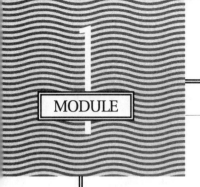

WORD PROCESSING

Objective:

WordPerfect is the industry standard word-processing package. Its adaptability to other application software and its relative ease of use makes it the most popular word-processing program available. To learn the advantages of WordPerfect, you need to comprehend the command functions used by WordPerfect. Let us now review several of WordPerfect's basic commands.

COMMAND FUNCTIONS

WordPerfect uses the function keys (F1–F10) in conjunction with the SHIFT, CTRL, and ALT keys to create commands. For your convenience, a template of the command structure is located in Appendix B. Accessing the commands is very simple. For example, if you want to bold the word Student, press the F6 key, type the word, and then press the F6 key again to turn off the bold. Similarly, the F8 key is used to underline text.

Example 1

Type the following letter as it is shown. Use the commands to bold (F6), under-line (F8), or format margins (SHIFT-F8) where possible. Do not correct any misspelled words.

```
        4 Hodgenville
        Irvine, CA 92720

        January 4, 1988

        Mr. Michael McLaughlin
        St. Ambrose University
        School of Business
        Davenport, IA 52220

        Dear Mr. McLaughlin:

        How would you like to hlp thousnds of our local high school
        students learn better business practices while getting some free
        publicity for your new book?

        You can do both of these things by spnding just an hour talking
        to the local business teachers at our annual conference. Luckily,
```

our meeting is schedled for August 8–10, the same time as the Academy of Management meeting here in nearby Anaheim. We would be glad to pay you an honorarium of $100 as well as provide transportation to and from your hotel. This opportunity to reach more than 15,000 students by addressing 150 teachers is one you'll truly enjoy.

Please call me collect at (714)651-8951 by January 23 to let me know the date you prfer and the topic of your talk. I am looking forward to talking to you.

Sincerely,

Steven Gillis
Conference Chair

Example 2

Make the following changes to the document. Compare your document with the document in Example 1 to insure accuracy.

1. Change the address to your address.

2. Change the university address to Wilkes University, Wilkes-Barre, PA 18766.

3. Use the Spell Checker (CTRL-F2) to check the spelling of the document.

4. Print (SHIFT-F7) and save the document (F10).

Solution

205 S. Franklin Street
Wilkes-Barre, PA 18766

January 4, 1988

Mr. Michael McLaughlin
Wilkes University
School of Business
Wilkes-Barre, PA 18766

Dear Mr. McLaughlin:

How would you like to help thousands of our local high school students learn better business practices while getting some free publicity for your new book?

You can do both of these things by spending just an hour talking to the local business teachers at our annual conference. Luckily, our meeting is scheduled for August 8–10, the same time as the Academy of Management meeting here in nearby Anaheim. We would be glad to pay you an honorarium of $100 as well as provide transportation to and from your hotel. This opportunity to reach more than 15,000 students by addressing 150 teachers is one you'll truly enjoy.

Please call me collect at (714)651-8951 by January 23 to let me know the date you prefer and the topic of your talk. I am looking forward to talking to you.

Sincerely,

Steven Gillis
Conference Chair

Word Processing Exercises

1. Create a letter similar to the letter in Exercise 1 that explains the advantages of using a word processor instead of a typewriter.

Moving Text

A frequently used feature of WordPerfect is its ability to move or copy text to different places within the document. This gives the user the added flexibility of altering the document after it has been created. To move or copy text, the following procedures must be followed:

- Move the cursor to the area the text is positioned.

- Press ALT-F4 (Block). This turns the blocking feature on so you can highlight the area you want to move or copy.

- Highlight the area you want to move or copy using the arrow keys.

- Press CTRL-F4 (Move). A menu will appear on the bottom. Select 1 (Block). The text that you highlighted will disappear from the screen. [Note: If you wish to copy the text, select 2 (Copy) instead of 1 (Block).]

- Move the cursor to the area you want the text to be located. Press RETURN to relocate the text.

2. Retrieve the sample letter created in Exercise 1. To retrieve the file, select SHIFT-F10 and type in the filename. When the file has been retrieved, move the second paragraph in front of the fourth. Then move it back to its original position.

3. A good way to learn many of the popular formatting functions of WordPerfect is to create a resume. Create a resume using the following sections: heading, objective, educational background, work experience, professional affiliations, and references. Utilize as many format commands as you can. Some of the commands to try are:

Format	Keys
Centering	SHIFT-F6
Bold	F6
Underline	F8
Margins	SHIFT-F8
Font	ALT-F8
Spell	CTRL-F2

When the resume is completed, save it under the filename RESUME and print the file.

Line Draw

Line Draw is a feature on WordPerfect that allows the user to draw vertical and horizontal lines within the document. In order to draw lines, follow the simple instructions.

- Select CTRL-F3 to enter the Line Draw menu.

- Select 2 (Line Draw).

- Select the style of line you wish to use. If you select 1, you will draw a single line.

- Draw lines wherever you want them to be placed. When you are finished, Select 6 to move without drawing lines. To begin drawing lines again, press the desired line style and begin drawing lines.

- If you wish to change the size of the line choose 4 and select one of the eight choices given or you can select your own style by selecting 9 and typing the character of your choice from the keyboard.

  After you feel confident with Line Draw, try Exercise 4.

4. Using the Line Draw feature, recreate the hierarchial chart below. [Hint: Type the text first and then draw boxes around the text.]

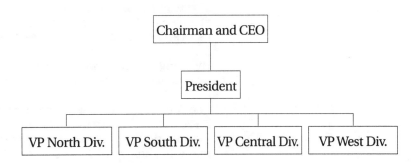

5. Using the Line Draw feature, recreate the data flow diagram below. [Hint: Type the text first and then draw boxes around the text.]

Loan Application Process

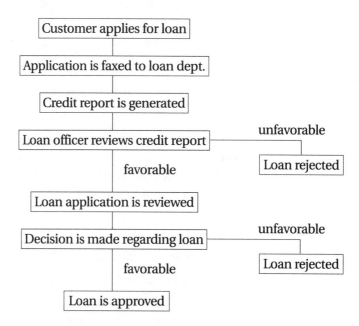

6. Input the following memo. With the skills you have now acquired, improve the appearance of the memo by utilizing the following WordPerfect features: bold, underline, centering, and spell checker.

MEMORANDUM

TO: Division Managers

FROM: John Smith

DATE: January 4, 1994

RE: Use of WordPerfect software

This memo is to inform you that XYZ, Inc. has decided to use WordPerfect as its standard word-processing package. This decision came after careful evaluation of the direct benefits XYZ, Inc. can receive from this software package.

By using only one word-processing package, XYZ's letters, manuals, memos, and reports will be generated with minimal difficulty.

The MIS department will coordinate the installation and training. XYZ, Inc. feels this package will solve the problem of software incompatibility because WordPerfect is fully compatible with many leading word-processing and spreadsheet packages.

If any department has any questions or concerns over this decision, please forward any comments to the MIS department.

Columns

A distinct advantage to WordPerfect is its ability to create columns of text. An example of this feature is a newspaper or periodical column. To create a column using WordPerfect, select ALT-F7-1. This will allow you to enter the Column Format menu. You then need to choose 1 to turn the Column feature on. WordPerfect will then take you back to the worksheet. To move between columns, choose CTRL-ENTER.

7. Create a newsletter using the Column feature. Include headings and titles where appropriate. A sample document using the Column feature is found below.

This document explains how the Column feature in WordPerfect works. The Column Format menu is chosen by pressing ATL-F7. Next you select 1 to enter the Column menu. Select 3 to define your column constraints. These may include the type of column, the number of columns, the distance between columns, and the column margins.

After you have established your criteria, you need to select 1 to turn the Column feature on. WordPerfect will then take you back to the worksheet and you may start typing in column 1. If you wish to move to the next column, simply hit CTRL-ENTER. If you want to stop the column, simply hit ENTER and the column mode will end.

If you have any questions about creating columns, refer to the help screen by pressing F3 twice and pressing ALT-F7 from the Template menu. Each subject described in this section will be fully explained.

As you can see, the Column Format can be very useful if you need to publish a newsletter or write a column.

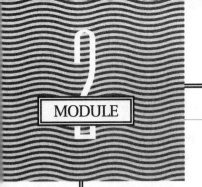

MODULE

SPREADHSEET ANALYSIS

Objective:

Lotus 1-2-3 is a highly versatile spreadsheet software package. This section will orient the user to some of the advanced features for manipulating data and working with Lotus 1-2-3 spreadsheets.

SPREADSHEET
ANALYSIS
EXAMPLES

Example 1

Build a repayment schedule for a $10,000.00 loan at 9% interest for 36 months.

Solution

Set up columns A–E with the column headings shown below. In column A use the /Data Fill command to enter payment numbers 0–36. Format columns B–E for currency using /Range Format Currency. Type in @PMT(10000,0.09/12,36) starting at payment 1, then copy the cell to all 36 payments. You must type in the following formulas in the corresponding columns.

$$\text{Interest} = \frac{\text{Previous Balance} \times \text{Interest}}{12}$$

Principal Repayment	= Monthly Payment − Interest
Remaining Balance	= Previous Balance − Principal Repayment

Output

PAYMENT NUMBER	MONTHLY PAYMENT	INTEREST	PRINCIPAL REPAYMENT	REMAINING BALANCE
0	$0.00	$0.00	$0.00	$10,000.00
1	$318.00	$75.00	$243.00	$9,757.00
2	$318.00	$73.18	$244.82	$9,512.18
⋮	⋮	⋮	⋮	⋮
⋮	⋮	⋮	⋮	⋮
⋮	⋮	⋮	⋮	⋮
36	$318.00	$0.00	$318.00	$0.00

Example 2

Star Manufacturing plans to purchase a new stamping machine. The machine costs $120,000.00 and has a life span of 11 years. To justify the capital expenditure, Star Manufacturing must decide to use straight-line depreciation or double-declining depreciation. Build a spreadsheet with depreciation calculated both ways for the life of the machine.

Solution

In columns A, B, and C type in the respective column headings.
`Year, Double-Declining Depreciation, Straight-Line Depreciation`.
In column B type in the following command for each year:

@DDB(COST,SALVAGE,LIFE,PERIOD)

Where: COST = Original cost of the machine
SALVAGE = Salvage value if any
LIFE = Life of the machine
PERIOD = The number of years for depreciation of the asset

In column C type in the following command for each year:

@SLN(COST,SALVAGE,LIFE)

Where: COST = Original cost of the machine
SALVAGE = Salvage value if any
LIFE = Life of the machine

Output

YEAR	DOUBLE DECLINING DEPRECIATION	STRAIGHT LINE DEPRECIATION
1	$21,818.18	$9,545.45
2	$17,851.24	$9,545.45
3	$14,605.56	$9,545.45
4	$11,950.00	$9,545.45
5	$9,777.28	$9,545.45
6	$7,999.59	$9,545.45
7	$6,545.12	$9,545.45
8	$5,355.10	$9,545.45
9	$4,381.44	$9,545.45
10	$3,584.82	$9,545.45
11	$1,131.68	$9,545.45

Example 3

Fullerton Brush Company gives out sales commissions according to the dollar amount of gross sales for every quarter. The company gives a 3% commission on sales less than $4,000.00/per quarter and a sales commission of 5% for sales greater than or equal to $4,000.00/per quarter. Using the data below determine the dollar amount and percentage of commission for each salesperson.

Solution

In the percent commission column use the formula,

@IF(1STQTR>=4000,.05,.3)

In the amount commission field use the formula,

@IF(1STQTR>=4000,1STQTR*.05,1STQTR*.03)

The general format for the @IF statement is,

@IF(CONDITION, TRUE, FALSE)

Salesperson	1st Qtr Sales	Percent Commission	Amount Commission
Joe Smith	$4,103.15	5.00%	$123.09
Jonathon Jones	$3,856.00	3.00%	$115.68
Marion Walters	$4,500.00	5.00%	$135.00
Ronald Smithers	$3,210.00	3.00%	$96.30
Sally Worth	$1,981.00	3.00%	$119.43

Spreadsheet Analysis Exercises

1. Calculate the double-declining and straight-line depreciation for a piece of equipment costing $150,000.00 and having a life of 13 years. At the end of its life the machine can be sold for $13,000.00.

2. A consumer needs to borrow $15,000.00 for a new car but can't decide on the payback period. Prepare two repayment schedules for the loan using an interest rate of 8.5% and terms of 36 months and 60 months for the customer. (See Example 1.)

3. The Hitech Inc. data-processing center bases its yearly raises partially on an input operator's error rate. The error rates are classified as Low, Medium, or High. Using the listed criteria below and the operator's error rates, print in column C the correct error rating for each operator.

LOW	=	0% to 2.0%
MEDIUM	=	2.1% to 4.0%
HIGH	=	4.1% >

Input Operator	Error Rate	Error Rating
Quincy Johnston	4.20%	
Carol Smith	2.50%	
Renee Jones	1.20%	
Mark Ashton	5.60%	
Gregory Davis	3.10%	
Andrew Withers	2.20%	
Maureen Wilson	1.60%	

Hint: Use a nested @IF statement,

@IF(ERRRATE>=.041,"HIGH",@IF(ERRRATE>=.021......))

4. A mall ice cream vendor wants to estimate the number of quarts of ice cream sold on any given day. The vendor has identified three independent variables that could affect his ice cream sales: hours of sunshine, average temperature, and number of buses in lot. How many quarts of ice cream can the vendor expect to sell on day 7 given the 3 independent variables?

Quarts Sold	Day	X1 Hours Of Sunshine	X2 Avg. Temp	X3 Buses In Lot
550	1	4.5	91	5
350	2	3.2	82	6
480	3	4.1	84	3
300	4	2.5	86	4
475	5	3.8	90	3
300	6	2.9	88	5
	7	4.0	85	4

Hint: Use the /DATA REGRESSION command to find a general prediction equation and then substitute DAY 7 values as follows:

PREDICTION DAY 7 = (X1COEFF*4)+(X2COEFF*85)+(X3COEFF*4)

5. A consulting firm has retained your services to determine the validity of starting one of three possible business ventures. They include: (1) a commercial textbook store, (2) a seven-cage outdoor batting facility, (3) a six-court indoor tennis facility.

Using your area as a test market select one of the three ventures for investigation. Using appropriate variables that determine assets and liabilities, prepare a cash flow analysis for the first three years of operations. This analysis should be comprehensive and complete so that it can be presented to a loan officer at the bank.

6. The accounting department wants you to set up a Lotus 1-2-3 spreadsheet to keep track of all bills paid per month. The spreadsheet should consist of the following fields: date, payee, bill total, invoice number, cost center, and comment. Build the spreadsheet and use a **macro** to tab between fields and accept input.

[Hint: The macro should look like this:
    {?}~{RIGHT}{?}~{RIGHT}{?}...ETC.]

Use the name \0 for the macro so that the macro is initiated automatically whenever the spreadsheet is retrieved.

STATISTICAL ANALYSIS

Objective:

Minitab is a statistical package that can be run in either batch or interactive mode. Minitab allows an analyst to perform a variety of statistical tasks including descriptive and inferential analyses.

STATISTICAL

ANALYSIS

EXAMPLES

Example 1: Measures of Central Tendency and Variabilities

Three salespersons have identified their volume of sales during each month of this past year. Compute the mean, median, and standard deviation of sales volume from the given data.

	Salesperson #1	*Salesperson #2*	*Salesperson #3*
January	5	8	6
February	7	7	3
March	6	10	2
April	4	6	0
May	2	5	5
June	0	8	4
July	10	11	6
August	3	3	0
September	6	4	2
October	2	6	1
November	1	7	3
December	3	5	4

Solution

```
MTB>     READ    INTO    C1-C3
DATA>      5       8       6
DATA>      7       7       3
DATA>      6      10       2
DATA>      4       6       0
DATA>      2       5       5
DATA>      0       8       4
DATA>     10      11       6
DATA>      3       3       0
DATA>      6       4       2
DATA>      2       6       1
DATA>      1       7       3
DATA>      3       5       4
DATA>  END
          12 ROWS READ

MTB > DESCRIBE C1-C3
```

	N	MEAN	MEDIAN	TRMEAN	STDEV	SEMEAN
C1	12	4.083	3.500	3.900	2.843	0.821
C2	12	6.667	6.500	6.600	2.348	0.678
C3	12	3.000	3.000	3.000	2.089	0.603

	MIN	MAX	Q1	Q3
C1	0.000	10.000	2.000	6.000
C2	3.000	11.000	5.000	8.000
C3	0.000	6.000	1.250	4.750

Example 2: Scatter plot

Plot the following data.

x	y
5	12
7	21
15	33
22	45
28	52

Solution

```
MTB>     READ INTO    C1-C2
DATA>        5          12
DATA>        7          21
DATA>       15          33
DATA>       22          45
DATA>       28          52
DATA> END
         5 ROWS READ
MTB> PLOT C1 VS C2
```

Part 1 Problem-Solving Modules

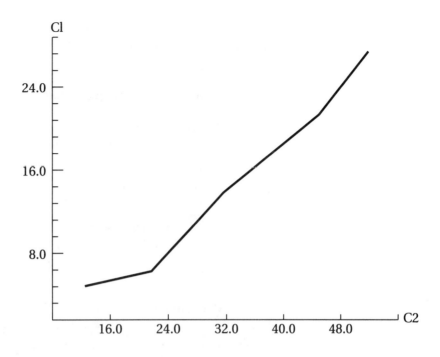

Example 3: Correlation Analysis

A banker wished to determine the relationship between percentage down payment (*x*) and the number of foreclosures per 100,000 loans (*y*). The data indicated the following:

x	*y*
10%	11
20%	4
30%	2
40%	1

Compute the correlation of the above data set.

Solution

```
MTB>     READ INTO   C1-C2
DATA>       .10        11
DATA>       .20         4
DATA>       .30         2
DATA>       .40         1
DATA> END
         4 ROWS READ
MTB> CORR C1 VS C2

Correlation of C1 and C2 = −0.916
```

Example 4: Linear Regression

Using the data given in Example 3, find

    A. the line of best fit $y = a + bx$

    B. the predicted number of foreclosures for a 25% down payment

Solution

```
MTB>     READ INTO   C1-C2
DATA>        .10         11
DATA>        .20          4
DATA>        .30          2
DATA>        .40          1
DATA> END
        4 ROWS READ
MTB> REGRESS C2 ON 1 INDEP VAR C1

The regression equation is C2 = 12.5 - 32.0 C1

Predictor        Coef        Stdev        t-ratio        p
Constant        12.500       2.711          4.61       0.044
C1             -32.000       9.899         -3.23       0.084

s = 2.214   R-sq = 83.9%   R-sq (adj) = 75.9%

Analysis of Variance

SOURCE          DF        SS          MS         F          p
Regression       1     51.200      51.200     10.45      0.084
Error            2      9.800       4.900
Total            3     61.000

Let  C3 = 12.5-32.0*.25

Print C3

4.5
```

Example 5: Multiple Linear Regression

An admissions counselor at a large urban university wanted to determine the best predictors of grade point average (y) as determined by IQ (x_1), Miller's Analogy Test (x_2), and GMAT scores (x_3).

GPA	IQ	MILLERS	GMAT
3.5	128	38	410
3.0	115	30	350
2.8	111	21	300
2.7	113	32	310
3.1	122	35	370
3.7	130	42	430
3.2	125	40	360
3.6	133	37	340

A. Find the multiple linear regression equation for the given data.

B. What variable is the best predictor of GPA?

Solution
A. $y = -2.70 + .0450C2 - .0210C3 + .00314C4$

B. IQ, since $r_{12} = .954$

Statistical Analysis Exercises

1. A manufacturing firm that produces tennis balls has three shifts of operation. The number of defective balls for a period of one week are given in the table.

SHIFT 1	SHIFT 2	SHIFT 3
50	22	36
35	16	59
22	18	73
81	43	62
53	29	44
65	31	55
74	43	39

A. Compute the mean, median, and standard deviation for the number of defects for each shift.

B. Which production shift has the smallest average of defective tennis balls?

2. Crime statistics were reported by 12 cities. The following frequencies of crime over twelve months were tabulated. Compute the mean, median, and standard deviation for each type of crime.

City	x (Felonies)	y (Petty Thefts)	z (Rapes)
1	220	545	12
2	100	200	5
3	110	350	8
4	490	992	15
5	140	260	1
6	380	740	2
7	205	410	1
8	195	320	1
9	245	645	2
10	150	800	2
11	310	720	7
12	540	860	20

3. Stock prices were listed for three computer stocks over a 6-month period.

Month	IBM	Apple	Hewlett Packard
1	55	22	60
2	62	24	65
3	75	30	70
4	63	26	72
5	71	28	80
6	80	25	85

Using the data plot each stock over the 6-month period. Which stock appears to have the greatest growth factor?

4. A real estate company wanted to determine which variables x_1 through x_3 are most important in predicting the cost of a home (y). The data is given in the table.

y (cost)	x_1 (sq. footage)	x_2 (age)	x_3 (acreage)
140,000	2000	5	1.5
175,000	2400	10	2.5
400,000	3500	20	3.0
200,000	2800	7	3.5
150,000	2100	12	3.0
180,000	1500	2	3.0
122,000	1700	4	2.0

A. Find the multiple linear regression line for the data.

B. Using the multiple linear regression line from part A, find the expected cost of a home (y) if the square footage is 2700 sq.ft., the age of the home is 8 years, and the acreage is 5.

C. Find the explained variance r^2 from the print-out. Does the r^2 value from this problem indicate a "good model?" (We shall define a good model as $r^2 > .60$.)

D. Does the model show any multicollinearity? (Multicollinearity is defined as a high correlation ($r \geq .60$) between the independent variables.)

5. Students taking a freshman course in psychology were queried about their grade point average (x) and their hours of study per week for this course (y). The data given in the table.

x	y
3.2	2
3.5	10
2.8	2
2.4	3
1.5	9

Compute the correlation coefficient for the data. Does the data indicate a good correlation between the two sets of values? (Assume that a value of $r \geq .6$ or $r \leq -.6$ indicates a good correlation.)

6. A local hospital wished to predict its bed usage over a 7-year period. The data in the table indicates their usage.

x *(year)*	y *(% of beds)*
1	.40
2	.62
3	.74
4	.63
5	.58
6	.37
7	.39

Using the mean function (e.g. mean of C2), compute the average percentage of bed utility over the two years that the hospital has been in operation. Sort the data, place the sorted data into C3, and print the sorted data. [Hint: (SORT C2 PLACE INTO C3) (PRINT C3)]

7. A hospital wished to study the relationship between the number of residence physicians on staff and their number of patients treated.

Physicians	Patients Treated
5	205
8	415
12	821
15	1020
22	1411
30	1811

Find a linear regression model for the data using patients treated as a dependent variable. Using the linear regression equation estimate the number of patients treated if the hospital utilizes the services of 25 physicians.

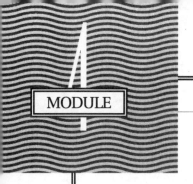

MARKOV ANALYSIS

Objective:

A **Markov chain** is a set of conditional or transition probabilities in which a future state of events is determined by the present state. The matrix representation of the probabilities is called a **transition matrix,** because the matrix determines the probability of moving from a present state to the next state. The transition matrix exhibits certain properties: 1) it is a square matrix; 2) all entries of probabilities must be greater than or equal to zero and less than or equal to one; and 3) the sum of all the given values in each row must equal one. Problems in this section utilize the CMMS software package.

MARKOV ANALYSIS EXAMPLES

Example 1

A small town has two competing florists, Flowerama (F) and Flower Station (FS). At the year's end it was determined that the two flower shops each had 50% of the town's business. During prior years it was found that Flowerama had retained 80% of their customers and had lost 20% of their customers to Flower Station. Flower Station managed to retain 70% of its customer base while losing 30% to Flowerama.

    A. Find the market share for the next seven years for each floral shop.

    B. Find the steady state or equilibrium market share for these two shops.

Solution

```
           −=*=− DATA INPUT  −=*=−

ENTER THE TOTAL NUMBER OF STATES
ENTER NUMBER IN RANGE (2−12) & press 2

ENTER NUMBER OF ABSORBING STATES
ENTER NUMBER IN RANGE (0−1) & press 0

DO YOU WANT TO RE-ENTER PROBLEM STRUCTURE? (Y/N)
Enter a character (Y or N) & press n

        −=*=− INFORMATION ENTERED  −=*=−

TOTAL NUMBER OF STATES      =  2
NUMBER OF ABSORBING STATES  =  0
```

```
                    TRANSITION TABLE

STATES      1       2
   1      0.800   0.200
   2      0.300   0.700

                MARKET SHARE PROBABILITIES

     SHARE
 1   0.500
 2   0.500

           MARKET SHARE ANALYZED FOR 7 PERIODS

                 −=*=− RESULTS  −=*=−

                STEADY STATE PROBABILITIES

      0.600   0.400

                 MEAN FIRST PASSAGE TIMES
 1   1.667   5.000
 2   3.333   2.500

                 FIRST PASSAGE TIME VARIANCES
 1   3.333   20.00
 2   7.778   11.25

                 EXPECTED RECURRENCE TIMES
      1.667   2.500

                  MARKET SHARE ANALYSIS

       MARKET SHARE AT THE BEGINNING OF EACH PERIOD

PERIOD                    STATE
 1        0.500   0.500
 2        0.550   0.450
 3        0.575   0.425
 4        0.588   0.412
 5        0.594   0.406
 6        0.597   0.403
 7        0.598   0.402
 8        0.599   0.401

            TRANSITION MATRIX AFTER PERIOD 7
 1        0.603   0.397
 2        0.595   0.405

       - - - - - E N D   O F   A N A L Y S I S - - - - -
```

Example 2

Suppose a third floral shop, Crossroads (C), enters into the picture and a new transition matrix becomes

	F	S	C
F	.8	.1	.1
S	.2	.7	.1
C	.1	.3	.6

The market share at the end of the first year was Flowerama 45%, Flower Station 30%, and Crossroads 25%.

    A. Find the market share for each floral shop at the end of five years.

    B. Find the steady-state market share for each floral shop.

Solution

```
                    —=*=— DATA INPUT  —=*=—

Do you want a Market Share Analysis?
Enter a Character (Y or N) & press y

Enter the number of periods for the market share
analysis
ENTER NUMBER IN RANGE (1-25) & press 5

              —=*=— INFORMATION ENTERED —=*=—

TOTAL NUMBER OF STATES       =  3
NUMBER OF ABSORBING STATES   =  0

                    TRANSITION TABLE

STATES    1         2         3
   1     0.800     0.100     0.100
   2     0.200     0.700     0.100
   3     0.100     0.300     0.600

                MARKET SHARE PROBABILITIES

     SHARE
 1   0.450
 2   0.300
 3   0.250

             MARKET SHARE ANALYZED FOR 5 PERIODS

                  —=*=— RESULTS  —=*=—

                STEADY STATE PROBABILITIES
     0.450   0.350    0.200

                  MEAN FIRST PASSAGE TIMES
 1   2.222   7.143   10.00
 2   5.556   2.857   10.00
 3   6.667   4.286    5.000
```

```
                  FIRST PASSAGE TIME VARIANCES
1   11.85     35.71    90.00
2   27.78     17.96    90.00
3   30.37     22.24    60.00

                  EXPECTED RECURRENCE TIMES
        2.222    2.857    5.000

                      MARKET SHARE ANALYSIS

        MARKET SHARE AT THE BEGINNING OF EACH PERIOD

PERIOD                              STATE
1         0.450   0.300   0.250
2         0.445   0.330   0.225
3         0.445   0.343   0.213
4         0.445   0.348   0.206
5         0.447   0.350   0.203
6         0.448   0.351   0.202

              TRANSITION MATRIX AFTER PERIOD 5
1         0.502   0.304   0.194
2         0.424   0.382   0.194
3         0.378   0.397   0.225

    - - - - - E N D   O F   A N A L Y S I S - - - - -
```

Markov Analysis Exercises

1. Consider a marketing analysis comparing Proctor & Gamble's Tide detergent with their leading competitor's product Surf. A study conducted using 100 consumers showed that 50% chose Tide and 50% chose Surf. Suppose that Tide retains 80% of its customer base but loses 20% to Surf. Surf retains 60% of its customers but loses 40 % to Tide.

    A. Find the market share of each product at the end of two years.

    B. Find the steady-state market share of each product.

2. An individual owns 100 shares of IBM stock and wishes to monitor the progress of his stock at the end of each month. At a month's end there are 3 possibilities for the stock: increase, drop, or unchanged. Assume that the following probabilities apply:

stock increases	= .6
stock decreases	= .3
stock unchanged	= .1

These probabilities can be summarized in the transition matrix

	Up	Unchanged	Down
Up	.6	.3	.1
Unchanged	.3	.4	.3
Down	.2	.4	.4

If on any given day there is an equal likelihood of either one of these three occurrences, find the steady-state probabilities for the three states of IBM stock.

3. Suppose that General Motors (GM), Ford (F), and Chrysler (C), each introduce a new minivan with mileage ratings in excess of 40 mpg. Assume that each company initially captures $\frac{1}{3}$ of the market. However, after the first year it was determined that GM retained 85% of its customers, but loses 10% to Ford and 5% to Chrysler. Ford kept 80% of its customers, but lost 10% to GM and 10% to Chrysler. Chrysler kept 60% of its customers, but lost 25% to GM and 15% to Ford. If these trends continue, determine

   A. the market share that each company will have at the end of three years.

   B. the steady-state market share for each firm.

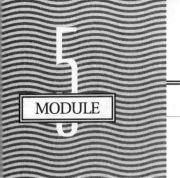

LINEAR PROGRAMMING

Objective:

Linear Programming was first introduced in 1947 when George Dantzig used the concepts of linear algebra for determining optimal solutions to problems involving restrictions (constraints). Linear programming utilizes a set of variables to maximize profits, minimize costs, or to optimize various productivity or allocation problems. All solutions assume non-negativity (e.g. $x, y \geq 0$). Problems in this section utilize the CMMS software package.

LINEAR PROGRAMMING EXAMPLES

Example 1

Maximize the function $z = 2x_1 + 8x_2$ subject to the constraints

$$3x_1 + 9x_2 \leq 45 \quad \text{and} \quad 2x_1 + x_2 \geq 12$$

Solution

```
            -=*=-INFORMATION ENTERED-=*=-

NUMBER OF VARIABLES        =   2
NUMBER OF <= CONSTRAINTS   =   1
NUMBER OF = CONSTRAINTS    =   0
NUMBER OF >= CONSTRAINTS   =   1
```

MAX PRFT $= 2x_1 + 8x_2$

SUBJECT TO: $3x_1 + 9x_2 \leq 45$
$2x_1 + x_2 \geq 12$

```
                -=*=-RESULTS-=*=-

VARIABLE       VARIABLE VALUE
```
x_1 4.2
x_2 3.6

OBJECTIVE FUNCTION VALUE: 37.2

Example 2

Minimize the function $z = 30x_1 + 3x_2$ subject to the following constraints:

$$5x_1 + x_2 \geq 10$$
$$x_1 + x_2 \leq 6$$
$$x_1 + 2x_2 \geq 6$$
$$x_1 < 4$$

Solution

```
        -=*=-  INFORMATION ENTERED  -=*=-

NUMBER OF VARIABLES        =  2
NUMBER OF <= CONSTRAINTS   =  2
NUMBER OF  = CONSTRAINTS   =  0
NUMBER OF >= CONSTRAINTS   =  2
```

MIN PRFT $= z = 30x_1 + 3x_2$

subject to: $5x_1 + x_2 \geq 10$
$\qquad\qquad x_1 + x_2 \leq 6$
$\qquad\qquad x_1 + 2x_2 \geq 6$
$\qquad\qquad\quad x_1 \leq 4$

```
            -=*=-RESULTS-=*=-
```

VARIABLE	VARIABLE VALUE
x_1	1.0
x_2	5.0

OBJECTIVE FUNCTION VALUE: 45

Linear Programming Exercises

1. Wilkes Lumber Company produces 3 types of plywood. The data in the table summarizes the production hours and profitability per unit of each of the three manufacturing operations. How many units of each grade of lumber should Wilkes produce?

Type of wood	Production (hours)			Profit/unit
	I	II	III	
Grade A	2	2	4	$20
Grade B	5	5	2	$30
Grade C	10	3	2	$40
Maximum Time Available	900	400	600	

2. IBM would like to determine how many units of PS/2 model 50 and PS/2 model 90 to manufacture for a future production period. Both models utilize the same Intel microprocessor. Assembly times are 3 hours for the PS/2 model 50 and 7 hours for the PS/2 model 90. IBM has 3500 microprocessors available for this production run and 8000 hours of assembly available. Management has specified that at least 40% of the production time should be for PS/2 model 50 computers. If the profitability per unit is $800 for the model 50 and $1200 for the model 90, how many units of each model should IBM manufacture?

3. Consider the following linear program: Minimize $z = 3x_1 + 48x_2$ subject to the constraints

$$x_1 + 3x_2 \geq 6$$
$$x_1 + x_2 \geq 4$$

Find the optimal solution.

4. Investment Associates (IA) manages stock portfolios for a select group of clients. A new client requested that IA handle a $100,000 investment portfolio. As an initial investment strategy the client would like to restrict the portfolio to a mix of the following stocks:

Stock	Price/Shr	Est. Ann. Rtn/Shr	Risk Index/Shr
Getty Oil	$30	$3	.50
Intel	$40	$5	.25
Walmart	$25	$2	.10

The risk index for a particular stock is a rating of the relative risk of the three investment alternatives. Thus, of the three stocks Getty Oil is considered to be the riskiest. By constraining the total risk IA lessens the overall risk of the portfolio. For the current portfolio an upper limit of 700 has been set for the total risk index of all investments. In addition, IA has set an upper limit of 1500 shares for the risky Getty Oil Stock. How many shares of each should be purchased in order to maximize the total annual return?

5. Solve the following linear programming problem: Maximize $2x_1 + 3x_2$ subject to the constraints

$$x_1 + 2x_2 \leq 6$$
$$5x_1 + 3x_2 \leq 15$$

PART 2

KNOWLEDGE-BASED MODULES

THE KNOWLEDGE-BASED MODULES WILL PROVIDE
APPLICATION EXERCISES USING VP-EXPERT AND
DBASE IV. THE EXERCISES IN THE VP-EXPERT
SECTION WILL HELP THE STUDENT UNDERSTAND HOW
PROBLEM SOLVING USING A COMPUTER RELIES ON FACTS
AND RULES TO FORM A CONCLUSION. THE COMPUTER
ALSO CAN BE PROGRAMMED TO USE HISTORICAL
INFORMATION TO FORM NEW CONCLUSIONS AS IN
ARTIFICIAL INTELLIGENCE SYSTEMS.

■

THE DBMS SECTION USES DBASE IV TO TEACH DATA
MANIPULATION AND DATABASE CREATION. IN THIS
SECTION STUDENTS WILL BE ASKED TO CREATE
DATABASES AND PROBLEM-SOLVING CODE USING
DBASE IV.

VP-EXPERT

Objective:

An expert system is a computer program that is able to make an unstructured or semi-structured decision that is often made by a human expert. One type of expert system is called a rule-based system. A rule-based system is comprised of two components, an inference engine and a knowledge base. The knowledge base stores the facts and rules regarding a particular domain of a subject. The inference engine contains the control strategy. It searches through the knowledge base and determines how the facts and rules are to be manipulated and processed. In essence the inference engine executes the reasoning needed to solve the problem. Application areas for expert systems include credit or loan applications, college admissions decisions, equipment diagnosis, and personnel training. Problems in this section utilize VP-EXPERT Software.

VP-EXPERT EXAMPLES

Example 1

Tenth National Bank has a policy governing the approval of loans. Loans are approved if the applicants' monthly bills are less than 25% of their monthly income. Build a rule for the inference engine that would help a manager make a loan approval decision.

Solution

```
RULE   LOAN_APPROVAL
IF     MONTHLY_BILLS < (.25*MONTHLY_INCOME)
THEN   POSSIBLE_EVENT = APPROVAL
ELSE   POSSIBLE_EVENT = NOT_APPROVED
```

Example 2

A college admits students based on an applicant's high school GPA and SAT score. Build a rule-based inference engine to determine whether or not each applicant fits the college's criteria.

Criteria   GPA >=3.0 and SAT >=800

Applicant	GPA	SAT
John Smith	3.5	950
Dale Thomas	3.2	840

Jane Ann Powlas	2.9	890
Carol Smythe	3.0	780
William Evans	2.7	810
Marilyn Jones	3.9	830

Solution

```
! A knowledge base to help determine possible appli-
  cants for
! college admittance
ACTIONS
CLS
DISPLAY "According to the data available, this ap-
plicant's approval is rated as {approval_rating}.";

RULE  GPA_TEST
IF    GPA = 3.0to4.0
THEN  APPROVAL_RATING = GOOD
ELSE  APPROVAL_RATING = NOT_GOOD;
RULE  SAT_TEST
IF    SAT = 800to900 OR
      SAT = 900>
THEN  APPROVAL_RATING = GOOD
ELSE  APPROVAL_RATING = NOT_GOOD;

ASK GPA:"What is the applicants GPA? " {GPA};
ASK SAT:"What is the applicants SAT score? " {SAT};

CHOICES GPA:1.0to2.0, 2.1to2.9, 3.0to4.0
CHOICES SAT:600to700, 701to799, 800to900, 900>
```

Output

```
Applicant            Approval Rating
John Smith             GOOD
Dale Thomas            GOOD
Jane Ann Powlas        NOT GOOD
Carol Smythe           NOT GOOD
William Evans          NOT GOOD
Marilyn Jones          GOOD
```

VP Expert Exercises

1. Northeastern University uses the following criteria to select candidates for its graduate program. Build an inference engine that will help the Admissions Department pick potential graduate students.

$$(GPA*GMAT) >= 1300 \quad and \quad SAT >= 800$$

	Undergraduate		
Applicant	GPA	GMAT	SAT
John Jones	3.8	450	800
Marilyn Lynnette	2.9	475	750
Dorothy Summers	3.5	500	810
Carol Rogers	3.75	550	850
Gregory Mantis	2.8	375	725
Mark Walters	3.9	590	785

2. Summerline Pools needs to hire 3 assembly line workers, and 35 people have applied for the job. The Human Resource Department has decided to interview all applicants that rate good or better in three areas: job knowledge, previous experience, and cost of necessary training. Build an inference engine that prompts the user to enter ratings for each area for each employee. Pick random ratings for the 35 employees and print out each user that gets a good to excellent rating. Use the following ratings.

Job Knowledge	Excellent	Good	Poor
Previous Experience	High	Medium	Low
Cost to Train	High	Medium	Low

3. First Western Bank is looking into ordering a new copier. All perspective copiers must rate well in three categories: quality of copies, speed, and ease of maintenance. Build an inference engine to pick all copiers with a good to excellent rating for the purchasing agent to consider. Enter the 10 ratings below to test your inference engine.

Copier	Quality	Speed	Ease
Model 1100	Good	Medium	High
System 1250	Excellent	Fast	Medium
Model IIa	Poor	Fast	Medium
Model 9000	Fair	Slow	Low
Model 150X	Good	Medium	Low
Turbo 2000	Fair	Fast	High
System 3500II	Excellent	Slow	Low
Model 3XII	Poor	Fast	High
Model IIIA	Good	Fast	Low
Model 5000V	Good	Slow	Medium

4. Klein, Smythe & Burnham Financial Services, Inc. has rated the top 10 mutual funds for risk, return, and management fees. They will only recommend funds that rate good to excellent. Build an inference engine that rates the 10 mutual funds below.

Fund	Risk	Return	Fees
Fidelity	Medium	High	Medium
20th Century	Low	Medium	High
Invesco	Low	Medium	Low
Templeton	High	Low	Medium
Vanguard	Medium	Medium	High
Dreyfus	Low	High	Low
Putnam	High	High	High
Janus	Low	Low	Low
Scudder	Medium	Low	High
Berger	High	High	Low

5. Western Manufacturing, Inc. is looking for a Plant Manager. Previous experience has shown that hiring from within yields greater employee loyalty and respect for the new manager. Three supervisors have applied for the position. These three persons are being rated on three areas from their last evaluations: leadership ability, delegation, and overall performance. Following are the ratings the three persons received. Build an inference engine to evaluate the best possible choice.

Supervisor	Leadership	Delegation	Overall Performance
Peggy Harding	Good	Sufficient	Good
John Williams	Excellent	Good	Good
William Jones	Poor	Good	Good

6. Mr. and Mrs. Jones are looking for a new house. Mr. and Mrs. Jones have two children, ages 7 and 9, and earn $80,000.00 a year collectively. They have decided to pick their house using the following criteria: square footage, land, proximity to a school, and price. Build an inference engine to pick out the best house for the Jones's.

House	Square Footage	Land (Acres)	Proximity to a School	Price
1	2200	.5	Yes	75,000.00
2	2600	1.0	Yes	99,000.00
3	2500	1.0	No	95,000.00
4	2000	1.5	No	99,000.00
5	3000	1.5	Yes	120,000.00
6	2800	1.5	No	110,000.00
7	2500	1.5	Yes	100,000.00

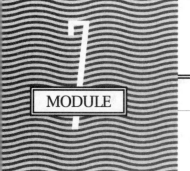

DBMS

Objective

This section deals with the subject of database management and its role in Decision Support Systems. The gathering and storage of data is vital to the daily operations and success of any organization, because much of the decision-making process is related to the data organizations receive. For example, past sales figures are one way of determining the demand for a particular item. Without accurate and timely data, a business simply cannot function in today's competitive business world.

This section is designed to give information about the fundamental concepts of a database system, show how a database system relates to Decision Support Systems, and introduce database programming using dBase IV. This section illustrates how a structured database system can alleviate many problems that occur in data storage and retrieval. Prior knowledge or the ability to learn dBase IV will greatly enhance understanding and appreciation of this topic.

DBMS EXAMPLES

Example 1

Create a database structure in dBase IV using the following fields:

Field Name	Field Type	Width	Dec
Customer	Character	15	
Ordernum	Numeric	6	
Orderdate	Date	8	
Amount	Numeric	7	2

Solution

At the dot prompt type in the word "create" as indicated below:

```
.CREATE
```

The user will then be given the following screen prompt:

```
ENTER THE NAME OF THE NEW FILE:
```

Enter the file name as CUSTOMER. Once the file name is selected, the user will see a data-entry screen identical to the format of the preceding table. Continue entering field names, types, and lengths according to the values shown in the previous table.

Example 2

Using the current database structure, enter the following 6 records:

Clevite	Gould	Helbig
160245	135422	142813
12/13/95	9/18/95	10/18/95
5005.25	2040.60	400.80

Milan	Towmotor	Waxman
172640	162431	112651
12/18/95	12/15/95	8/14/95
8455.60	3225.40	6425.35

1. Save the records by entering CTRL-END or ALT-E-S.

2. Generate a list of the records entered.

Solution

To display the records in your file enter the following command:

```
.LIST
```

The entire contents of your file should appear on the screen as follows:

CUSTOMER	ORDERNUM	DATE	AMOUNT
CLEVITE	160245	12/13/95	5005.25
GOULD	135422	9/18/95	2040.60
HELBIG	142813	10/18/95	400.80
MILAN	172640	12/18/95	8455.60
TOWMOTOR	162431	12/15/95	3225.40
WAXMAN	112651	8/14/95	6425.35

DBMS Exercises

1. Safeguard Financial Services wishes to produce a report that lists the account number, customer name, and balance due of its delinquent customers.

A. Write a report having the following format

Safeguard Financial Services

Account Number	Customer Name	Balance Due	Phone Number
XXXXXX	XXXXXXXXXX	9999.99	XXXXXXX
XXXXXX	XXXXXXXXXX	9999.99	XXXXXXX
.	.	.	.
.	.	.	.
XXXXXX	XXXXXXXXXX	9999.99	XXXXXXX

B. Using the structure developed in part *A*, print out the above report using the following data

Account Number	Customer Name	Balance Due	Phone Number
50216	Zilch	762.00	8432181
53182	Mann	63.00	2478219
11543	Gordon	642.25	6632183
18141	Seeley	2543.28	6663121
21432	Frail	421.75	6762142

C. Print out the report only for the accounts having a balance due greater than $500.00.

3. Develop a program using dBase IV that determines the optimal investment of the following three choices.

$13,000 investment at 7% fixed for 5 years
$15,000 investment at 5% fixed for 2 years
$9,000 investment at 15% fixed for 10 years

Use the simple interest formula for your calculations. [Hint: Define each variable and plug the variables into the formula.]

This type of program can be developed on the command line. Its purpose is to illustrate how dBase IV evaluates numerical data. For example, to determine the first investment choice type the following lines at the dot prompt.

```
PRINCIPAL=13000 ↵
RATE=.07 ↵
TIME=5 ↵
?=(PRINCIPAL*RATE*TIME)+PRINCIPAL ↵
```

4. Suppose an individual has a gross income of $50,000, and his taxable income is in the 35% tax bracket. Use dBase IV to create a program that will accept the variables and compute the individual's tax and net income.

5. You are a retail bank manager working with the marketing department on developing new products and services for retail bank customers. The target market for the new products has been established as customers with a deposit of $10,000 or more. You have requested the Information Services Division to develop a program to sort the main database to retrieve a list of target customers having assets of $10,000 or more.

A. What fields would be important to include in the search (for example, account number, and balance)?

B. Using the command mode create a database file with fields you feel are important for a bank to store. (Note: The record layout must contain an account and balance field.) Create a file of 20 records having at least 10 records showing a balance of over $10,000. [Hint: To create a database file in the command mode, type Create <filename > and press return. Creating a file in assist mode accomplishes the same task.]

C. Using the command mode, list the accounts with balances of $10,000 or more. The list should include the customer name, the account number, and the balance amount.

6. You are a customer service manager for a department store. The store manager wants to create an automated database of customer complaints in order to respond more effectively to complaints. The manager decides to use a database application to store the customers personal information and information regarding the complaint. However, the employees are not proficient with computers. The manager, therefore wants you to develop an application that will enable the employees to enter the information with ease and with little chance of making errors. Using dBase IV, develop a complete database application that would be useful in this situation, keeping in mind the need for simplicity and accuracy of data entry. The application should include a report feature for management to track complaints and a screen for data entry.

7. An owner of a small, mail-order business needs a database system to input customers orders, produce daily sales reports to management, and track the order and payment process. You have been hired as a consultant to develop the system, train employees on the system, and monitor any problems the system may encounter.

   A. Outline a proposal to the management of this company. Identify any constraints that may occur in the initial development of the system.

   B. Develop the logical design of the system. This should include a data flow diagram and pseudo-code identifiable with a dBase IV program.

8. You are beginning a small, mail-order business. You need to develop a database system for your operators to accept orders from customers and print invoices for each order.

   A. Develop a complete database program that accepts orders from customers. The screen generator should be utilized.

   B. Create a report that will print the customers full name, address, and order information. The report writer should be utilized.

   C. Create a report that will print a daily activity of all orders processed.

   [Note: A database applicable to this scenario will need to be created.]

Discussion Questions

1. What other ways could dBase IV be used to aid in decision making for management?

2. Do you notice any similarities or differences in the dBase IV coding with other database languages?

3. Is dBase IV a fully functional relational database?

PART 3

PROGRAMMING LANGUAGES MODULES

THE PROGRAMMING LANGUAGE MODULES WILL

PROVIDE APPLICATION EXERCISES IN COMPUTER

PROBLEM SOLVING USING THE BASIC,

PASCAL, FORTRAN, COBOL, AND SQL

LANGUAGES. STUDENTS WILL BE EXPECTED TO

PERFORM THESE EXERCISES USING THE

ESSENTIAL FEATURES OF EACH PROGRAMMING

LANGUAGE. EACH PROGRAM SHOULD BE FULLY

DOCUMENTED AND UTILIZE ONE OR MORE OF

THE THREE TYPES OF PROGRAM STRUCTURES:

SEQUENCE, SELECTION, AND LOOPING.

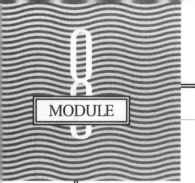

BASIC PROGRAMMING

Objective:

BASIC is an acronym for Beginner's All-Purpose Symbolic Instruction Code and represents a teachable English-like programming language. Students are encouraged to write well documented and accurate programs in this section.

BASIC PROGRAMMING EXAMPLES

Example 1

Write a BASIC computer program that inputs three data values and computes their average.

Solution

```
REM THIS PROGRAM COMPUTES THE
REM AVERAGE OF 3 NUMBER X1, X2, X3.
READ X1, X2, X3
DATA 50, 20, 5
AVERAGE = (X1+X2+X3)/3
PRINT 'AVERAGE = ', AVERAGE
STOP
```

Output

```
AVERAGE = 25
```

Example 2

The metric system is used for weight and measurement computations. Using the following conversions write a BASIC computer program that converts 50 miles to its appropriate metric equivalent in centimeters, meters, and kilometers.

1 inch	=	2.54 centimeters
1 foot	=	.3048 meters
1 mile	=	1.61 kilometers

Solution

```
REM THIS PROGRAM CONVERTS 50 MILES
REM INTO ITS CORRESPONDING METRIC
REM EQUIVALENTS IN CENTIMETERS, METERS,
```

```
REM AND KILOMETERS
READ MILES
DATA 50
CMS = MILES*5280*12*2.54
METERS = MILES*5280*.3048
KMS = MILES*1.61
PRINT '50 MILES =' CMS ' CENTIMETERS'
PRINT '50 MILES =' METERS ' METERS'
PRINT '50 MILES =' KMS ' KILOMETERS'
```

Output
```
50 MILES = 8,046,720 CENTIMETERS
50 MILES = 80,467 METERS
50 MILES = 80.50 KILOMETERS
```

BASIC Programming Exercises

1. A statistics professor wishes to compute the average of five test scores for each of three students. The following scores were recorded. Write a computer program that will identify each student, his/her scores, and his/her average grade.

Student 1	95	84	78	72	84
Student 2	88	76	78	91	86
Student 3	75	79	86	93	81

2. First Eastern Bank of Pennsylvania likes to provide financial tables for their customers. Management would like to have tables showing monthly payments on auto loans ranging from 36 to 60 months. Each table should give the payments for loans ranging from $1,000 to $20,000 in increments of $1,000. Using the formula:

$$M = \frac{AI(I + N)N}{(1 + I)N}$$

where: A is the amount of the loan, I is the monthly loan rate expressed as a decimal ($R/12$), R is the rate of interest, and N is the term of the loan. Write a BASIC program which will print the following table using interest rates of 8%, 9%, and 10%.

First Eastern Auto Loan
Payment Schedule for 1994

Interest Rate: xx *percent*

Loan Amount	Term of Loan (Months)			
	24	36	48	60
$xx,xxx	xxx.xx	xxx.xx	xxx.xx	xxx.xx

3. A graduate student is asked to demonstrate to his class the effect of compounding interest on the value of an investment. Compute the value of an investment of $5,000 over a term of ten years at 8% interest utilizing the formula:

$$A = P\left(1 + \frac{R}{N}\right)KN$$

where: P is the principal, R is the interest rate expressed as a decimal ($R/100$), K is the term of the investment, and N is the number of times compounding takes place per year.

Write a BASIC program to compute the value of the initial investment with compounding occurring 1, 4, 12, and 365 times per year. Output should appear as follows.

Times per Year Compounded	Investment Value
1	$x,xxx.xx
4	$x,xxx.xx
12	$x,xxx.xx
365	$x,xxx.xx

4. Write a BASIC computer program that prints your name, address, and phone number in the following format.

Last Name, First Name
Street Address
City, State, Zip Code
(Area Code) Phone Number

5. Write a BASIC computer program that accepts as input a part number, a quantity of each part purchased, and the total number of parts in stock and then computes the total sales. Suppose we are given the following data.

Part Number	Quant. Purch.	Units in Stock	Cost per Part
2053	20	100	45
1062	10	50	20
7621	100	335	10
6321	40	55	75

A. Find the total bill for the purchase of the four parts when the quantities indicated were purchased.

B. Print a new table in the identical format but reflecting the adjustment to the existing inventory.

6. Using the formula, $I = Prt$ where: I = interest, P = principal, r = rate, t = time in years. Write a computer program in BASIC that will compute the interest on a principal of $1,000.00 invested for 5 years having an interest rate of 6%.

7. An alumnus leaves $250,000.00 to a university's scholarship fund. If the university invests the money at an annual interest rate of 8%, how many $5,000.00 scholarships can it give in the donor's name? Assume that only dollars generated from interest can be used for scholarships, thus always retaining the initial endowment of $250,000.00. Use the formula for computing simple interest.

8. Write a BASIC computer program which computes the values of:

   A. $N!$ where $N = 5$.

   B. $_NP_R = N!/(N - R)!$ where $N = 7$ and $R = 3$.

   C. $_NC_R = N!/R!(N - R)!$ where $N = 6$ and $R = 4$.

   [Note: $N! = N \cdot (N-1) \cdot (N-2) \ldots 3 \cdot 2 \cdot 1$]

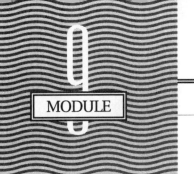

PASCAL Programming

Objective:

PASCAL is a higher level programming language that is explicitly concerned with structured programming. Syntax rules encourage the use of constructions and practices that are associated with the creation of clear and reliable programs. The general form of a PASCAL program must take the following form.

PROGRAM

  name of program;

CONSTANT

  constant definition;

    "   "

    "   "

    "   "

  constant definition;

VARIABLE

  variable declaration;

    "   "

    "   "

    "   "

  variable declaration;

BEGIN

  program statement;

    "   "

    "   "

    "   "

  program statement;

END

PASCAL PROGRAMMING EXAMPLES

Example 1

Write a PASCAL computer program that inputs an employee's hours worked and rate of pay. Compute the employee's gross pay and net pay if he works 40 hours and earns $7.50/hour. (A flat tax rate of 27% is to be assumed.)

Solution

```
PROGRAM PAYROLL;

CONST
    TAX = .270;

VAR
    HOURS, RATE, GROSS, NET: REAL;

BEGIN
    WRITELN ('ENTER HOURS WORKED AND RATE OF PAY ');
    READLN (HOURS, RATE);
    GROSS := HOURS*RATE;
    NET := GROSS*(1-TAX);
    WRITELN (' GROSS = $' ,GROSS, 'NET = $' ,NET)

END
```

Output

```
GROSS = $300.00 NET = $219.00
```

Example 2

Write a PASCAL computer program that computes the area of a circle having a radius of 12 inches. Use pi = 3.14.

Solution

```
PROGRAM AREA;

CONST
    PI = 3.14;

VAR
    AREA, RADIUS:REAL;

BEGIN
    WRITELN ('ENTER RADIUS OF CIRCLE');
    READLN (RADIUS);
    AREA := PI*RADIUS**2;
    WRITELN ('AREA = ',AREA)

END
```

Output
```
AREA = 452.16
```

PASCAL Programming Exercises

1. Write a PASCAL computer program that computes the area of a triangle with sides $A=5$, $B=12$, and $C=13$. Use the formula

$$K = S(S-A)(S-B)(S-C) \text{ where } S = \frac{1}{2}(A+B+C)$$

2. A company employs eight salespersons. Their commissions for each of the six weeks rounded to the nearest dollar are $525, $650, $480, $625, and $750. Write a PASCAL computer program that determines the sum of the commissions and the average weekly commission.

3. Write a PASCAL computer program that reads a stock price and converts it to its decimal equivalent (e.g., the program should convert $25\frac{1}{2}$ to 25.5). Use the program to display the following table.

Stock	Price	Decimal Equivalent
IBM	$80\frac{3}{4}$	XX.XX
Southwest	$16\frac{5}{8}$	XX.XX
Walmart	$25\frac{1}{4}$	XX.XX
Xerox	$39\frac{7}{8}$	XX.XX

4. Using the following data, write a program that reads up to 10 utility bills, sorts the bills in ascending order, and totals the bills.

Customer	Utility Bill
A	40.25
B	155.73
C	28.62
D	58.73
E	101.62
F	79.23
G	88.26
H	73.42
I	43.28
J	62.91

5. Joe Zilch has a checking account with City Bank Corp. Joe's account number is 100178 and beginning in January his balance was $6,000.00. Write a PASCAL computer program to display the following:

Account number is 999999
Depositor name is xxx xxxxx
Beginning balance $999,999.99

The program also should include the check numbers, dates, transaction of the following debits and/or credits, and ending balance as shown.

Date	Check Number	Transaction	Balance
10/05/94	125	−482.00	
10/12/94	126	−823.00	
10/22/94	Deposit	300.00	
10/25/94	127	−1126.00	

Output

The balance after four transactions is _____ .

6. Bank Ohio advertises that its savings accounts pay $6\frac{1}{4}\%$ interest compounded quarterly. Bank One pays $6\frac{1}{8}\%$ interest compounded daily. Which of the two financial institutions provides the best return on your money? Write a PASCAL computer program that computes the effective interest rate for each of the two investments using the formula,

$$r_e = \left(1 + \frac{r}{n}\right)^n - 1$$

where: r = annual rate of interest, n = number of times of compounding/year, and r_e = effective interest rate.

7. The formula for computing compound interest is

$$A = P\left(1 + \frac{r}{m}\right)^{mt}$$

where: P = principal
  r = rate of interest expressed as a decimal
  t = number of years of investment
  m = number of times interest is compounded/year

A total of $10,000 is invested at a rate of interest of 6%. Write a PASCAL computer program that computes the worth of the investment after a 10-year period if interest is compounded (a) quarterly, (b) monthly, (c) daily.

8. Write a PASCAL computer program that inputs two sets of coordinates (X_1, Y_1) and (X_2, Y_2) and finds

A. the slope of the line segment connecting the 2 points
($m = (Y_2 - Y_1) / (X_2 - X_1)$, where m is the slope of the line).

B. The midpoint (X, Y) of the line segment joining the two points
(X_1, Y_1) and (X_2, Y_2) where

$$X = \frac{(X_1 + X_2)}{2}$$

$$Y = \frac{(Y_1 + Y_2)}{2}$$

C. Using $(X_1, Y_1) = (2,6)$, $(X_2, Y_2) = (4,12)$, and the programs from
parts A. and B., compute the slope and midpoint of the line
joining these two points.

9. Given the following matrices

$$A = \begin{bmatrix} a_{11} & a_{12} \\ a_{21} & a_{22} \end{bmatrix}, \quad B = \begin{bmatrix} b_{11} & b_{12} \\ b_{21} & b_{22} \end{bmatrix},$$

Write a PASCAL computer program that computes the following.

A. The sum of 2 matrices as defined by

$$A + B = \begin{bmatrix} a_{11} & a_{12} \\ a_{21} & a_{22} \end{bmatrix} + \begin{bmatrix} b_{11} & b_{12} \\ b_{21} & b_{22} \end{bmatrix} = \begin{bmatrix} a_{11} + b_{11} & a_{12} + b_{12} \\ a_{21} + b_{21} & a_{22} + b_{22} \end{bmatrix}$$

B. The determinant of any 2×2 matrix where the determinant is
defined as

$$a_{11}a_{22} - a_{12}a_{21}$$

C. Test your equations in parts A and B using

$$A = \begin{bmatrix} 1 & 3 \\ 4 & 6 \end{bmatrix} \quad \text{and} \quad B = \begin{bmatrix} 2 & 4 \\ 6 & 1 \end{bmatrix}$$

FORTRAN PROGRAMMING

Objective:

FORTRAN is a mathematical and scientific programming language that continues to be used extensively. Programs written in this section should be compatible with either the FORTRAN 77 or FORTRAN 90 compilers. Students will be expected to write correct and well-documented programs.

FORTRAN PROGRAMMING EXAMPLES

Example 1

Write a FORTRAN computer program that reads in two rates of speed, 20 mph and 30 mph, and computes a harmonic mean using the formula

$$m_h = \frac{N}{1/X_1 + 1/X_2}$$

where: N = the number of rates of speed and X_1, X_2 are the rates of speed

Solution

```
C     THIS PROGRAM COMPUTES A HARMONIC MEAN
      DATA N/2/,X1/20/,X2/30/
      M = N/(1/X1 + 1/X2)
      PRINT 'THE HARMONIC MEAN IS ', M
      STOP
      END
```

Output

```
THE HARMONIC MEAN IS 24
```

Example 2

Write a FORTRAN program which computes the expected value of the top face of a die where the expected value is equal to the sum of the products of each random variable times its probability.

$F(X_i)$	.166	.166	.166	.166	.166	.166
$X = X_i$	1	2	3	4	5	6

Solution

```
C       THIS PROGRAM COMPUTES THE
C       EXPECTED VALUE OF THE TOP
C       FACE OF A DIE.
C       VARIABLES IN THIS PROBLEM INCLUDE
C       N = PAIRS OF DATA
C       X = VALUES OF THE RANDOM VARIABLE
C       F(X) = PROBABILITY OF EACH RANDOM VARIABLE
        DIM X(10), FX(10)
        DATA N/6/,FX/6*.166/,X(1)/1/,X(2)/2/,X(3)/3/,X(4)/4/
       *X(5)/5/,X(6)/6/
        EXPVAL = 0.0
        DO I=1,N
        EXPVAL = X(I)*FX(I)+EXPVAL
        PRINT *,EXPVAL = ,EXPVAL
        STOP
        END
```

Output

```
EXPVAL = 3.4999
```

FORTRAN Programming Exercises

1. Given the following data set which indicates a major baseball team's earned run average (x) and their number of games won (y) during a particular season.

x	y
2.25	96
3.54	63
3.12	73
2.89	68
2.72	82
2.54	78

Using Pearson's Product Moment Correlation r, given by the formula

$$r = \frac{N \, \Sigma xy - \Sigma x \Sigma y}{\sqrt{[N\Sigma x^2 - (\Sigma x)^2] \cdot [N\Sigma y^2 - (\Sigma y)^2]}}$$

Write a FORTRAN computer program to find the value of r.
[Hint: The value of r must be such that $-1 \le r \le 1$.]

2. Using the following data set indicating the relationship between student grade point average (y) and student IQ (x).

x	y
120	3.8
95	2.1
110	2.9
115	2.7
111	2.4
130	3.9
122	3.5

Write a FORTRAN program which will determine the point estimators a and b of the regression line $y = a + bx$. Use the formulas

$$b = \frac{N\Sigma xy - \Sigma x\Sigma y}{N\Sigma x^2 - (\Sigma x)^2},$$

$$a = \frac{\Sigma y}{N} - b\left(\frac{\Sigma x}{N}\right),$$

for finding the point estimators.

3. Write a general FORTRAN program that will read in the elements of an $m \times n$ matrix and sums the elements of each of the m rows and each of the n columns. A local bank reported the number of new customers at each of their four different branch offices during their first year of operation:

Branch Office	1st	2nd	3rd	4th
	QUARTER			
A	20	22	35	40
B	15	12	8	10
C	8	6	14	22
D	16	25	20	32

Write a FORTRAN computer program that totals the number of new customers for each branch and displays the total number of new customers for each quarter.

4. Two cities are 10 miles apart. A car leaves from the first city and averages 20 mph. The car then returns from the second city at an average speed of 30 mph. Find the average speed of the automobile using the equation

$$M_h = \frac{N}{1/R_1 + 1/R_2 + \cdots + 1/R_N}$$

where N = number of speeds and $R_1, R_2, ..., R_N$ = speeds.

5. An employee, on her 25th birthday, places $2,500.00 into a retirement fund that pays 7.5% interest compounded annually. Write a

FORTRAN computer program that will compute the money available in the employee's retirement fund at age 62.

6. Using the formula

$$A = P\left(1 + \frac{r}{m}\right)^{mt}$$

where: P = principal
r = rate of interest expressed as a decimal
t = number of years of investment
A = amount (in dollars) after t years
m = number of times interest is compounded/year

Write a FORTRAN computer program which will compute A (also known as the future value) for a $5,000.00 investment earning 10% interest for 20 years and is compounded annually.

7. Given the following set of 6 elements write a program that

A. sorts the set in ascending order

B. sorts the set in descending order

12
4
62
25
9
86

8. Write a FORTRAN computer program that reads in three resistances $R_1 = 50$, $R_2 = 100$, and $R_3 = 200$ and computes their combined resistance for a parallel circuit given by the formula

$$R = \frac{1}{1/R_1 + 1/R_2 + 1/R_3}$$

9. Write a FORTRAN computer program to generate the first 10 terms of the Fibonacci Series 1, 1, 2, 3, 5 ...

10. Write a program which inputs the lengths of two sides of a right triangle and solves for the hypotenuse. Test your program with $a = 5$ and $b = 12$. [Hint: $a^2 + b^2 = c^2$.]

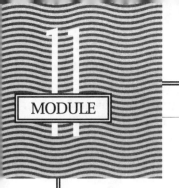

COBOL Programming

Objective:

COBOL is an acronym for Common Business Oriented Language. The objective of this section is to familiarize the reader with the basic and advanced programming techniques used in COBOL for analyzing data that would be useful in managerial decision making. This section also assumes a basic knowledge of the COBOL programming language.

COBOL PROGRAMMING EXAMPLES

Example 1

A sales company is deciding to implement a commission-based salary system, but top management can't decide the amount of the commission. The president is considering percentages of 5% to 7%. Write a COBOL computer program using the sales figures for five salespersons, calculating what the company would have to pay in sales commissions using the given percentages.

	Monthly Sales
Salesman 1	**$5,000.00**
Salesman 2	**$6,750.00**
Salesman 3	**$5,575.00**
Salesman 4	**$7,890.00**
Salesman 5	**$6,900.00**

Output

```
            Monthly Sales
                                5%          6%          7%
Salesman #1    $5,000.00     $250.00     $300.00     $350.00
Salesman #2    $6,750.00     $337.50     $405.00     $472.50
Salesman #3    $5,575.00     $278.75     $334.50     $390.25
Salesman #4    $7,890.00     $394.50     $473.40     $552.30
Salesman #5    $6,900.00     $345.00     $414.00     $483.00
                           $1,605.75   $1,926.90   $2,248.05
```

Example 2

Federated Foods, Inc. has decided to establish a customer service hotline. The company receives approximately 1,200 calls per day which are currently handled by the secretarial staff and clerks. Most calls last for 4 minutes with 1 minute between calls. Write a COBOL computer program to determine how many clerks Federated Foods will have to hire to handle all of the calls.

Use the formula

$$\text{Number of clerks} = \frac{N}{M/t}$$

where: N = number of calls/day

M = minutes per 8-hour shift less 1.5 hours for lunch and breaks

t = time for each call (4 minutes + 1 minute between calls)

N = 1,200
M = $(8 - 1.5) * 60$ = 390 minutes
t = 5 minutes

Number of clerks = 1200/(390/5)

Number of clerks = 15.38

Output

```
Number of clerks needed = 16.
```

[Hint: The number must be rounded up to accommodate all calls.]

COBOL Programming Exercises

1. Top management needs a report of the five largest customers of their products for a special promotion. Determine the five largest customers by adding up the individual sales and sorting the customers by total sales in descending order.

	Product			
Customer	*Power Saws*	*Hammers*	*Wrenches*	*Miscellaneous*
Acme Metals	$150.00	$300.00	$200.00	$100.00
Central Dist.	$300.00	$400.00	$75.00	$625.00
Eastern Supply	$900.00	$375.00	$400.00	$50.00
Main Hardware	$875.00	$150.00	$510.00	$862.00
Lefty's	$348.00	$1,300.00	$238.00	$560.00
West End Supply	$400.00	$600.00	$340.00	$818.00
Supply's-R-Us	$300.00	$650.00	$210.00	$900.00
National Dist.	$500.00	$120.00	$125.00	$195.00
Penn Supply	$320.00	$700.00	$650.00	$100.00
Joe's Warehouse	$625.00	$555.00	$750.00	$900.00

2. Metro Mailing wants to send sales brochures to all of its customers outlining new price changes. Before the mailing labels are printed, the Information File Manager needs to verify the information in the customer database. Write a program to read each record in the database verifying that there are no blank fields. A record with a blank field should be printed out so it can be corrected before the mailing.

The database structure is as follows.

Field	Type	Length
Name	A	25
Address1	X	25
City	A	15
State	A	2
Zip	9	9

3. At First National Bank, we approve your application for a loan based partially on your debt-to-earnings ratio. If this ratio is lower than 35%, you are considered a possible loan candidate. Use the given information to determine which applicants are eligible for loans.

	Monthly Income	Monthly Debt
Joe Smith	$1,500.00	$300.00
Carol Jones	$2,500.00	$825.00
Molly Wallace	$1,250.00	$462.50
Lisa Kay	$2,350.00	$916.50
Mark Topps	$2,200.00	$748.00
Billy Evans	$1,300.00	$390.00
James Bud	$2,750.00	$875.00
Heather Prince	$1,975.00	$675.00

4. Data Processing, Inc. requires that each of its operators processes a minimum of 1100 items per hour. The firm pays an incentive on all items processed over this minimum according to the following criteria.

Items/Hour	Incentive
1101–1200	$1.00 for every 10 items
1201–1300	$2.00 for every 10 items
1301–1400	$3.00 for every 10 items
1401–1500	$4.00 for every 10 items
1501–1600	$5.00 for every 10 items
1601 or greater	$6.00 for every 10 items

Write a COBOL computer program to calculate the incentive pay for each operator listed.

Operator	Items/Hour
Joann Smith	1210
Melissa Jones	1430
John Wesson	1520
Wayne Wolfe	1380
Laurie Rogo	900
Paul Bath	1290
Mark Meredith	1470
Corrinne Thomason	1340
Lisa Schmuger	1601

An example is

Operator	Items/Hour
Gregory Smith	1480

$$\text{Incentive} = \frac{1480 - 1110}{10} * \$4.00 = \$152.00$$

5. Magic Notions, Inc. can save money by having its employees' pay deposited into their bank accounts instead of issuing checks. To do this, the bank requires a sequential file with each employee's account number and pay. Using the following employee records, create a file that Magic Notions could submit to the bank. Assume a flat tax rate of 24% to calculate net pay (hours over 40 earn time and a half).

Employee	Account	Hourly Wage	Hours Worked
William Jones	0916604	$8.50	40
Samantha Stevens	0916213	$9.25	36
Chuck Wooly	1235589	$7.35	45
Madison Smith	9885621	$10.15	38
Jane Haley	5546124	$8.25	41
Melissa Davis	6218594	$7.95	52
James Stewart	1258946	$8.55	40

6. Write a COBOL computer program that would be useful in the operation of a car rental company. The program should prompt and accept input for

A. Customer's name, address, phone number

B. Car type (compact, mid-size, full-size)

C. Car Manufacturer (Ford, Toyota, etc.)

D. Starting and ending rental dates

SQL PROGRAMMING

Objective

SQL is a computer language designed to process and query relational databases. It was developed in the mid-1970s under the name SEQUEL at the IBM San Jose research facilities as the data manipulation language for IBM's prototype relational model DBMS, System R. In 1980, it was renamed SQL (Structured Query Language) to avoid confusion with an unrelated hardware product called SEQUEL. SQL is the data manipulation language for IBM's current product offerings in the relational DBMS arena, SQL/DS and DB2. Retrieving data from the database is the most common SQL operation. A database retrieval is called a query and to issue a query you start with the SELECT command. The basic form of an SQL command has 3 parts or clauses:

SELECT	....**<column>**
FROM	....**<tables>**
WHERE	....**<restrictions>**

The entire SQL language consists of less than thirty commands. To execute SQL commands, the user must enter the instruction SET SQL ON in the dBase IV dot prompt mode. To exit from SQL type in SET SQL OFF and return to the dBase IV command line.

SQL is freeform. Using SQL the user can create, retrieve, and modify data from tables. A relational model appears to be just a collection of tables. These tables are called relations which explains how the relational model received its name. Relationships are established through linkage of common columns in two or more tables.

SQL PROGRAMMING EXAMPLES

CREATING A TABLE FILE

Example 1

```
CREATE TABLE EMPLOYEE
(EMPLOYEE PIDM NUMBER(8)       NOT NULL
EMPLOYEE_ID   CHAR(9)          NOT NULL
EMPLOYEE_LAST_NAME CHAR(60)    NOT NULL
EMPLOYEE_FIRST_NAME CHAR(15),
EMPLOYEE_MI   CAR(2),
EMPLOYEE_ENTITY_ID CHAR(1));
```

ADDING DATA TO THE TABLE FILE

Example 2

```
INSERT INTO EMPLOYEE
  VALUES(123132,'182650892','WILLIAMS',
  'CHRISTY','M','P');

INSERT INTO EMPLOYEE
  VALUES(345345,'999999999','SCHWARTZ',
  'RONALD','D','P');

INSERT INTO EMPLOYEE
  VALUES(678678,'888888888','GEORGE',
  'KENNETH','G','P');

INSERT INTO EMPLOYEE
  VALUES(901901,'777777777','ROSS',
  'JENNIFER','I','P');

INSERT INTO EMPLOYEE
  VALUES(487396,'111111111','BOMBER',
  'MARK',' ','P');
```

QUERYING TABLES WITH SELECT

SELECT	<columns>
FROM	<tables>
WHERE	<restrictions>

Example 3

```
SELECT EMPLOYEE_ID,EMPLOYEE_LAST_NAME
FROM    EMPLOYEE
WHERE   EMPLOYEE_PIDM = 123123;
```

Output

```
EMPLOYEE_LAST_NAME     EMPLOYEE_ID
Williams               182640892
```

Compound Conditions are formed by connecting two or more simple conditions using AND, OR, and NOT.

Example 4

```
SELECT EMPLOYEE_ID,EMPLOYEE_LAST_NAME,
       EMPLOYEE_FIRST_NAME,EMPLOYEE_MI
FROM    EMPLOYEE
WHERE   EMPLOYEE_LAST_NAME = 'Bomber'
AND     EMPLOYEE_MI IS NULL;
```

Both simple conditions must be true in order for the compound condition to be true. Null means there was no data in the EMPLOYEE_MI field.

Output

```
ID          LAST_NAME    FIRST_NAME   MI
111111111   Bomber       Mark
```

Example 5

When you use the '*' asterisk in place of actual column names, all column names are listed.

```
SELECT  *
FROM    EMPLOYEE
```

Output

```
PIDM     ID          LAST NAME   FIRST NAME   MI   ENTITY  ID
123123   182640892   Williams    Christy      M    P
345345   999999999   Schwartz    Ronald       D    P
678678   888888888   George      Kenneth      G    P
901901   777777777   Ross        Jennifer     I    P
487396   111111111   Bomber      Mark              P
```

COMPARISON OPERATORS

In the previous example the = sign was used as a statement of equality. There are many other comparison operators.

Example 6

```
SELECT  EMPLOYEE_ID,EMPLOYEE_LAST_NAME,
        EMPLOYEE_FIRST_NAME
FROM    EMPLOYEE
WHERE   EMPLOYEE_LAST_NAME LIKE 'R%'
AND     EMPLOYEE_FIRST_NAME LIKE 'J%';
```

Output

```
ID          LAST NAME   FIRST NAME
777777777   Ross        Jennifer
```

SORTING

Sorting is done by adding the ORDER BY clause which the user can request so that the results are displayed in any given order.

Example 7

```
SELECT *
FROM   EMPLOYEE
ORDER BY EMPLOYEE_LAST_NAME
```

Output

```
PIDM    ID         LAST NAME  FIRST NAME  MI  ENTITY ID
487396  111111111  Bomber     Mark            P
678678  888888888  George     Kenneth     G   P
901901  777777777  Ross       Jennifer    I   P
345345  999999999  Schwartz   Ronald      D   P
123123  182640892  Williams   Christy     M   P
```

The default is always ascending order. The results can be sorted in descending order by,

```
SELECT *
FROM EMPLOYEE
ORDER BY EMPLOYEE_LAST_NAME DESC;
```

CALCULATIONS

Calculations can be completed with a SELECT statement.

Example 8

Using the data in the Customer Table, find the available credit for all customers who have a credit limit of at least $800.00.

Customer Table

Cust Numb	Cust Name	Cust Addr	Balance	Cred lim	Slsr numb
124	Adams, Sally	481 Oak St	418.75	500	3
256	Samuels, Ann	215 Pete Ave	10.75	800	6
311	Charles, Don	48 College Dr	200.10	300	12
315	Daniels, Tom	914 Cherry St	320.75	300	6
405	Williams, Al	519 Watson	201.75	800	12
412	Adams, Sally	16 Elm St	908.75	1000	3
522	Nelson, Mary	108 Pine St	49.50	800	12
567	Baker, Joe	808 Ridge	201.20	300	6
587	Roberts, Judy	512 Pine St	57.75	500	6
622	Martin, Dan	419 Chip Dr	575.50	500	3

```
SELECT  CUSTNUMB, CUSTNAME,
        (CREDLIM-BALANCE)
FROM    CUSTOMER
WHERE   CREDLIM >= 800;
```

Output

CUSTNUMB	CUSTNAME	EXP1
256	Samuels, Ann	789.25
405	Williams, Al	598.25
412	Adams, Sally	91.25
522	Nelson, Mary	750.50

SQL has built-in functions to calculate such things as SUMS, MAX, MIN, and COUNTS.

Example 9

Using the Customer Table, count how many customers have a credit limit of at least $500.00.

```
SELECT  COUNT(CUSTNUMB)
FROM    CUSTOMER
WHERE   CREDLIM >= 500;
```

Output
```
COUNT(CUSTNUMB)
       7
```

Example 10

Find the total number of customers and the sum of their balances.

```
SELECT  COUNT(CUSTNUMB), SUM(BALANCE)
FROM    CUSTOMER
```

Output

COUNT(CUSTNUMB)	SUM(BALANCE)
10	2944.80

Example 11

Find the largest credit limit awarded to any customer of sales representative 3.

```
SELECT  MAX(CREDLIM)
FROM    CUSTOMER
WHERE   SLSRNUMB = 3;
```

Output

```
MAX(CREDLIM)
    1000
```

UPDATING DATA IN THE DATABASE

Example 12

Change the name of customer 256 in the Customer Table to 'Jones, Ann'.

Customer Table

Cust Numb	Cust Name	Cust Addr	Balance	Cred lim	Slsr numb
124	Adams, Sally	481 Oak St	418.75	500	3
256	Samuels, Ann	215 Pete Ave	10.75	800	6
311	Charles, Don	48 College Dr	200.10	300	12
315	Daniels, Tom	914 Cherry St	320.75	300	6
405	Williams, Al	519 Watson	201.75	800	12
412	Adams, Sally	16 Elm St	908.75	1000	3
522	Nelson, Mary	108 Pine St	49.50	800	12
567	Baker, Joe	808 Ridge	201.20	300	6
587	Roberts, Judy	512 Pine St	57.75	500	6
622	Martin, Dan	419 Chip Dr	575.50	500	3

```
UPDATE CUSTOMER
SET    CUSTNAME = 'Jones, Ann'
WHERE  CUSTNUMB = 256;
```

Output

```
CUST  CUST                                          CRED  SLSR
NUMB  NAME           ADDR           BALANCE  LIM   NUMB
124   Adams, Sally   481 Oak St      418.75   500    3
256   Jones, Ann     215 Pete Ave     10.75   800    6
311   Charles, Don   48 College Dr   200.10   300   12
315   Daniels, Tom   914 Cherry St   320.75   300    6
405   Williams, Al   519 Watson      201.75   800   12
412   Adams, Sally   16 Elm St       908.75  1000    3
522   Nelson, Mary   108 Pine St      49.50   800   12
567   Baker, Joe     808 Ridge       201.20   300    6
587   Roberts, Judy  512 Pine St      57.75   500    6
622   Martin, Dan    419 Chip Dr     575.50   500    3
```

DELETING DATA FROM A DATABASE

Example 13

Delete the customer named Al Williams from the Customer Table in Example 12.

```
DELETE CUSTOMER
      WHERE CUSTNAME = 'Williams, Al';
```

Output

CUST NUMB	CUST NAME	CUST ADDR	BALANCE	CRED LIM	SLSR NUMB
124	Adams, Sally	481 Oak St	418.75	500	3
256	Jones, Ann	215 Pete Ave	10.75	800	6
311	Charles, Don	48 College Dr	200.10	300	12
315	Daniels, Tom	914 Cherry St	320.75	300	6
412	Adams, Sally	16 Elm St	908.75	1000	3
522	Nelson, Mary	108 Pine St	49.50	800	12
567	Baker, Joe	808 Ridge	201.20	300	6
587	Roberts, Judy	512 Pine St	57.75	500	6
622	Martin, Dan	419 Chip Dr	575.50	500	3

SQL Programming Exercises

1. Using SQL, create the following 2 tables in the database called CUSTOMER. The table names should be Loan Table and Credit Table, respectively.

```
                Loan Table

CUSTOMER—SSNUM          CHAR(11)
CUSTOMER—LAST_NAME      CHAR(30)
CUSTOMER—FIRST_NAME     CHAR(15)
CUSTOMER—MI             CHAR(2)
CUSTOMER—LOAN_ID        CHAR(8)
CUSTOMER—LOAN_AMT       NUMERIC(6,0)


                Credit Table

CUSTOMER—LAST_NAME      CHAR(30)
CUSTOMER—FIRST_NAME     CHAR(15)
CUSTOMER—MI             CHAR(2)
CUSTOMER—SSNUM          CHAR(11)
CUSTOMER—LOAN_ID        CHAR(8)
CUSTOMER—CR_BAL         NUMERIC(6,0)
```

2. Using the Loan Table in Exercise 1, enter the following data.

```
INSERT INTO CUSTOMER
   VALUES ('288-40-5601','DAVIS','JAY','M','204162',80000);

INSERT INTO CUSTOMER
   VALUES ('273-21-4801','SEELEY','ROB','D','602413',100000);

INSERT INTO CUSTOMER
   VALUES ('243-26-3824','SNYDER','ROBIN','M','432184',60000);

INSERT INTO CUSTOMER
   VALUES ('261-43-2642','WELCH','WILLIAM','A','341286',50000);

INSERT INTO CUSTOMER
   VALUES ('234-42-1413','GREEN','BRYAN','A','321643',22000);

INSERT INTO CUSTOMER
   VALUES ('123-45-6789','SMITH','JIM','E','254564',35000);
```

3. Using the Credit Table in Exercise 1, enter the following data.

```
INSERT INTO CUSTOMER
   VALUES ('288-40-5601','DAVIS','JAY','M','204162',90000);

INSERT INTO CUSTOMER
   VALUES ('273-21-4801','SEELEY','ROB','D','602413','110000);

INSERT INTO CUSTOMER
   VALUES ('243-26-3824','SNYDER','ROBIN','M','432184',50000);

INSERT INTO CUSTOMER
   VALUES ('261-43-2642','WELCH','WILLIAM','A','341286',45000);

INSERT INTO CUSTOMER
   VALUES ('234-42-1413','GREEN','BRYAN','A','321643',30000);
```

4. **A.** Create a view named View1 that lists the following fields from the 2 tables.

   SSNUM, LNAME, FNAME, MI, LOAN_ID, LOAN_AMT, CR_BAL

   B. Create a view named View2 that lists customers' accounts that contain a higher loan amount than credit balance.

   C. Create a view named View3 that lists customers' accounts that meet the credit balance requirements.

SQL COMMANDS

KEY TO SYNTAX AND NOTATION

brackets [ ]	Item within brackets is optional
braces {|}	Enter the items separated by the	
ellipses . . .	Preceding items may be repeated several times
parentheses (,)	Parentheses and commas should be typed
underline ___	Default value
expr	Any expression consisting of column names and constants separated by arithmetic operation (+, −, /, and *)

DATA DEFINITION COMMANDS

```
ALTER TABLE TABLE {ADD | MODIFY} (column [NULL |
      NOT NULL],...);

CREATE [UNIQUE] INDEX name
      ON TABLE (column [ASC | DESC], column [ASC |
      DESC],...);

CREATE TABLE TABLE (column [NOT NULL],...);

CREATE TABLE TABLE [(COLUMN [NOT NULL],...)]
      [AS query];

CREATE VIEW NAME [ (alias,alias,...) ] AS query
      [WITH CHECK OPTION];

DROP {INDEX INDEX [ON TABLE] | TABLE TABLE | VIEW
      VIEW};
```

DATA MANIPULATION AND RETRIEVAL COMMANDS

```
DELETE FROM TABLE [WHERE condition];

INSERT INTO TABLE [(column, column,...)]
      {VALUES (value, value,...) | query ];

SELECT [ALL | DISTINCT] {[TABLE] * | expr, expr, ...}
      FROM TABLE [alias], TABLE [alias],...
      [WHERE condition]
      [GROUP BY expr, expr,...] [HAVING condition]
      [(UNION | INTERSECT | MINUS} SELECT...]
```

```
[ORDER BY {expr | position} [ASC | DESC],
 {expr | position} [ASC | DESC]...};
```

[Note: ORDER BY and FOR UPDATE OF clauses are valid only in SELECT commands, not in subqueries.]

```
UPDATE TABLE [ALIAS]
      SET column = expr, column = expr,...
      [WHERE condition];
```

OPERATORS USED IN SQL COMMANDS

VALUE OPERATORS

Operator	Function
( )	Overrides normal operator precedence rules
+, −	Prefix sign for a numerical expression
*, /	Multiplication and division
+, −	Addition and subtraction
‖	Character concatenation

LOGICAL OPERATORS

Operator	Function
( )	Overrides normal operator precedence rules
=	Test for equality
! = ∧ = | < >	Test for inequality
> | >= | < | <=	Greater than, greater than or equal to; less than, less than or equal to
NOT IN	Not equal to any member of; equivalent to '!=ALL'
IN	Equal to any member of; equivalent to '=ANY'
ANY	Compares a value to each value returned by a list or subquery
ALL	Compares a value to every value returned by a list or subquery
BETWEEN x and y	Greater than or equal to x, and less than or equal to y
EXISTS	True if a subquery returned at least one row
LIKE	Matches following pattern: '%' matches any sequence of characters, and '_' matches any single character
IS NULL	Column value is null
NOT	Reverses a logical expression's result; the following operators can be used: NOT BETWEEN, NOT EXISTS, NOT LIKE, NOT NULL
AND	Combines logical expressions to be true if both are true

OR	Combines logical expressions to be true if either is true

QUERY EXPRESSION OPERATORS

Operator	Function
UNION	Combines queries to return all distinct rows returned by either query individually
INTERSECT	Combines queries to return all distinct rows returned by both queries individually
MINUS	Combines queries to return all distinct rows returned by first query but not the second query

GROUP FUNCTIONS

Operator	Function
AVG ([DISTINCT] expr)	Average value of expr (null values ignored)
COUNT (DISTINCT expr I *)	Counts instances (ignoring nulls); COUNT(*) does not ignore nulls
MAX ([DISTINCT] expr)	Maximum value of expression (null values ignored)
MIN ([DISTINCT] expr)	Minimum value of expression (null values ignored)
SUM ([DISTINCT] expr)	Sum of values (null values ignored)

MISCELLANEOUS COMMANDS

```
Recovery
    ROLLBACK [WORK]
    COMMIT [WORK]
```

SECURITY

AND ACCESS

CONTROL

COMMANDS

```
GRANT [privilege, privilege,...| All}
ON TABLE
TO {user, user,...| PUBLIC}
[WITH GRANT OPTION];

REVOKE {privilege | ALL} ON TABLE
FROM {user, user,...| PUBLIC};
```

[Note: Privilege is one of: SELECT | INSERT | DELETE | UPDATE (column-list)]

RESERVED

WORDS

COMMANDS

[Note: Reserved words cannot be used as identifiers.]

ALL	EXISTS	OR
AND	FETCH	ORDER
ANY	FLOAT	PASCAL
AS	FOR	PLI
ASC	FORTRAN	PRECISION
AUTHORIZATION	FOUND	PRIVILEGES
AVG	FROM	PUBLIC
BEGIN	GO	REAL
BETWEEN	GOTO	ROLLBACK
BY	GRANT	SCHEMA
CHAR	GROUP	SECTION
CHARACTER	HAVING	SELECT
CHECK	IN	SET
CLOSE	INDICATOR	SMALLINT
COBOL	INSERT	SOME
COMMIT	INT	SQL
CONTINUE	INTEGER	SQLCODE
COUNT	INTO	SQLERROR
CREATE	IS	SUM
CURRENT	LANGUAGE	TABLE
CURSOR	LIKE	TO
DEC	MAX	UNION
DECIMAL	MIN	UNIQUE
DECLARE	MODULE	UPDATE
DELETE	NOT	USER
DESC	NULL	VALUES
DISTINCT	NUMERIC	VIEW
DOUBLE	OF	WHENEVER
END	ON	WHERE
ESCAPE	OPEN	WITH
EXEC	OPTION	WORK

WORDPERFECT TEMPLATE

	SHIFT	CTRL	ALT
F1	Cancel	Setup	Shell	Thesaurus
F2	--> Search	<--Search	Spell	Replace
F3	Help	Switch	Screen	Reveal Codes
F4	-->Indent	-> Indent <-	Move	Block
F5	List Files	Date/Outline	Text In/Out	Mark Text
F6	Bold	Center	Tab Align	Flush Right
F7	Exit	Print	Footnote	Columns/Table
F8	Underline	Format	Style	Font
F9	End Field	Merge Codes	Merge/Sort	Graphics
F10	Save	Retrieve	Macro Define	Macro

LOTUS 1-2-3 COMMANDS

FILE CREATION

Commands are accessed by activating the Lotus menu with the / key or by clicking the first letter of the command with the mouse.

Create new file	File New
Open existing file	File Open, type or select name
Save file	File Save
Save file with new name	File Save As, type name
Close file and window	File Close
Print spreadsheet	Select Area, File Print, select options
Undo last action	ALT-BACKSPACE or Edit Undo
Get context-sensitive help	Choose command, F1
Get function help	@-F1
Get macro help	{-F1
Look at Help Index	Help Index
Look at a Help topic	Click on one of the highlighted words
Leave Help	File Exit; or ALT-F4
Leave 1-2-3	File Exit; or ALT-F4

MOVING AROUND THE SPREADSHEET

Go to cell, range, or open file	Click on the cell, or F5, type address or selected range or file
Move left/right one screen	CTRL-LEFT or SHIFT-TAB CTRL-RIGHT or TAB
Move up/down one screen	PAGE UP/PAGE DOWN
Go to first non-blank cell	END-UP/END-DOWN
Go to next blank cell	END-RIGHT/END-LEFT

Go to last non-blank cell	END-HOME	
Go to cell A1	HOME	

ENTERING	Align label left	Begin with ' (apostrophe)
INFORMATION	Align label right	Begin with "
	Center label	Begin with ^
	Repeat label to fit a cell	Begin with \
	Display range names	Type formula or function, F3
	Display @functions	@-F3
	Display macro commands	{-F3
	Enter a date	Type date in a 1-2-3 date format or use @date(yy,mm,dd) and format it
	Enter a time	Type time in a 1-2-3- time format or use @time(hh,mm,ss) and format it
	Make address absolute	Type address, F4 (keep pressing F4 for variations)

EDITING	Start editing	F2 or click on right half of the edit bar
INFORMATION	End editing	ENTER or click on check mark button
	End editing without change	ESC-ESC or click on check mark button
	Delete character to right	DELETE
	Delete character to left	BACKSPACE
	Erase edit area	ESC
	Go to left end of entry	HOME
	Go to right end of entry	END
	Move five characters left/right	CTRL-LEFT/CTRL-RIGHT
	Toggle insert/ overtype modes	INSERT

	Find/replace characters	Select range, **Edit Find**, type characters, select Find/Replace with, type replacement characters, select Labels/Formulas/Both, select Find next/Replace/ Replace all

RANGE FUNCTIONS

	Erase range	Select range, DELETE, or **Edit Clear**
	Define range name	Select range, **Range Name Create**, type name

FORMATTING

	Format numbers and formulas	Select range, **Range Format**, select type, enter number of decimal places
	Change font/ style	Select range, **Style Font**, select font/style
	Align text in cell	Select range, **Style Alignment**, select type
	Align text over range	Select range, **Style Alignment**, **Align Over** range, Left/Center/Right/Even

PRINTING

	Preview printed worksheet	Select range, **File Preview**
	Compress work- sheet to fit page	**File Page** setup, select automatically fit to page

GRAPHING

	Create new graph	Select range, **Graph New**, type name
	Change graph type	**Chart Type**, select type, display, orientation
	Add title(s)	**Chart Headings**, type title(s)
	Add legend	**Chart Legend**, type range legend(s)
	Add graph to worksheet	Select worksheet range, **Graph Add** to sheet, select graph

MACROS

	Name macro	Select starting cell of macro, **Range Name Create**, type name
	Run macro	ALT-F3, select macro name
	Stop macro	CTRL-BREAK-ESC

Macros named with the \ (backslash key) followed by a single letter can be run by holding down CTRL and pressing the single letter.

MINITAB COMMANDS

NOTATION		
	K	Denotes a constant such as 4.3 or K17
	C	Denotes a column, such as 'age' or C8
	E	Denotes either a constant or a column
	[ ]	Encloses an optional argument

Lowercase letters indicate that word is not part of the command. Words written in lowercase may be omitted. Subcommands are shown indented under the main command.

GENERAL INFORMATION

HELP	Explains MINITAB commands
INFO	Gives status of the worksheet
STOP	Ends the current session
ABORT	A subcommand that cancels a command
PAPER	Output to printer
NOPAPER	Output to terminal only
RESTART	Begin fresh MINITAB session

ENTERING NUMBERS

READ	data [from 'FILENAME'] into C . . . C
SET	data [from 'FILENAME'] into C . . . C
INSERT	data [from 'FILENAME'] at end of C . . . C
END	of data *(optional command)*
RETRIEVE	the MINITAB worksheet saved [in 'FILENAME']
NAME	C='NAME_1', C='NAME_2', . . . , C='NAME_N'

OUTPUTTING NUMBERS

PRINT	the data in E . . . E
WRITE	[to 'FILENAME'] the data in C . . . C
SAVE	[in 'FILENAME'] a copy of the worksheet

EDITING AND MANIPULATING DATA

INSERT	data [from 'FILENAME'] between rows K, K of C . . . C
DELETE	rows K . . . K of C . . . C
COPY	columns C . . . C into C . . . C
ERASE	E . . . E
CODE	(K . . . K) to K for C . . . C stored in C . . . C
STACK	E . . . E stored in C
SUBSCRIPTS	to be stored in C
UNSTACK	C into E . . . E
SUBSCRIPTS	in C

You can also use LET to correct a number in the worksheet. Examples:

LET C2(3) = 42 *(third entry in column 2 is 42)*

LET C7(5) = '*' *(fifth entry in column 7 is missing)*

ARITHMETIC AND MATHEMATICAL FUNCTIONS

LET E = Mathematical expression

Mathematical expressions may use the arithmetic operators:

+, −, *, /, ** (raised to the power)

and any of the following functions:

ABS	**EXPO**	**MIN**	**SIN**
ACOS	**LAG**	**N**	**SORT**
ANTILOG	**LOGE**	**NMISS**	**SQRT**
ASIN	**LOGTEN**	**NSCORE**	**SSQ**
ATAN	**MAX**	**RANK**	**STDEV**
COS	**MEAN**	**ROUND**	**SUM**
COUNT	**MEDIAN**	**SIGNS**	**TAN**

COLUMN AND ROW OPERATIONS

The following are all done columnwise.

COUNT	Count the number of values in C [put into K]
N	(Number of nonmissing values) in C [put into K]
NMISS	(Number of missing values) in C [put into K]
SUM	Sum of the values in C [put into K]
MEAN	Mean of the values in C [put into K]
STDEV	Standard deviation of the values in C [put into K]
MEDIAN	Median of the values in C [put into K]
MINIMUM	Minimum of the values in C [put into K]
MAXIMUM	Maximum of the values in C [put into K]
SSQ	(Uncorrected sum of sq.) for C [put into K]

The following are all done rowwise.

RCOUNT	of E ... E put into C
RN	of E ... E put into C
RNMISS	of E ... E put into C
RSUM	of E ... E put into C
RMEAN	of E ... E put into C
RSTDEV	of E ... E put into C
RMEDIAN	of E ... E put into C
RMINIMUM	of E ... E put into C
RMAXIMUM	of E ... E put into C
RCOUNT	of E ... E put into C

PLOTS AND HISTOGRAMS

```
HISTOGRAM    C...C
DOTPLOT      C...C
BOXPLOT      C
```

HISTOGRAM, DOTPLOT, and BOXPLOT have subcommands:

```
INCREMENT = K
START at K [end at K]
BY C
SAME scale for all columns

STEM-and-leaf display of C...C
    TRIM outliers
    INCREMENT = K
    BY C
    PLOT C vs. C

MPLOT C vs. C and C vs. C and ... and C vs. C
```

PLOT and MPLOT have subcommands:

```
YINCREMENT = K
YSTART at K [end at K]
XINCREMENT = K
XSTART at K [end at K]
```

BASIC STATISTICS

```
DESCRIBE C...C
        BY C
```

ZINTERVAL	[K% confidence] assuming sigma=K for C ... C
ZTEST	[of mu=K] assuming sigma=K on data in C ... C
ALTERNATE = K	
TINTERVAL	[K% confidence] for C ... C
TTEST	[of mu=K] on data in C ... C

	ALTERNATE = K	
	TWOSAMPLE	test and c.i. [K% confidence] samples in C . . . C
	TWOT	test and c.i. [K% confidence] data in C, groups in C

TWOSAMPLE and TWOT have subcommands

ALTERNATE = K	
POOLED	
procedure	

REGRESSION	CORRELATION	between C . . . C
	REGRESS	C on k predictors C . . . C
AND		[store standardized residuals in C [fits in C]]
	NOCONSTANT	in equation
CORRELATION	COEFFICIENTS	put into C
	PREDICT	for values in E,E, . . . ,E
	RESIDUALS	put into C (observed − fit)

ANALYSIS OF	AOVONEWAY	analysis of variance for samples in C . . . C
	ONEWAY	analysis of variance, data in C, subscripts in C
VARIANCE		[store residuals in C [fits in C]]
	TWOWAY	analysis of variance, data in C, subscripts in C,C
		[store residuals in C [fits in C]]
	ADDITIVE	
	model	

NON-	RUNS	test [above and below K] for C
	SINTERVAL	sign c.i. [K% confidence] for C . . . C
PARAMETRIC	STEST	sign test [median = K] for C . . . C
	ALTERNATIVE	
STATISTICS	= K	
	WINTERVAL	Wilcoxon c.i. [K% confidence] for C . . . C
	WTEST	Wilcoxon signed-rank test [median=K] for C . . . C
	ALTERNATIVE	
	= K	
	MANN-	test and confidence interval [alternative = K]
	WHITNEY	[K% confidence] samples in C and C
	KRUSKAL-	test for data in C, subscripts in C
	WALLIS	

TABLES	CHISQUARE	test on table stored in C . . . C
	TABLE	the data classified by C . . . C
	MEANS	for C . . . C
	MEDIANS	for C . . . C
	SUMS	for C . . . C
	STDEV	for C . . . C
	N	for C . . . C
	COUNTS	
	ROWPERCENT	
	COLPERCENT	
	TOTPERCENT	
	TALLY	tallies the data in C . . . C
	COUNTS	
	PERCENTS	
	CUMCOUNTS	cumulative counts
	CUMPERCENTS	cumulative percents
	ALL	four of the statistics above

SORTING	SORT	C [carry along C . . . C] put into C [and C . . . C]
	RANK	the values in C, put ranks into C

DISTRIBUTION	SAMPLE	K rows from C . . . C put into C . . . C
	RANDOM	K observations into C . . . C
AND	PDF	for values in E [store results in E]
	CDF	for values in E [store results in E]
RANDOM DATA	INVCDF	for values in E [store results in E]

RANDOM, PDF, CDF, and INVCDF all have subcommands:

BERNOULLI	trials p = K
BINOMIAL	n = K, p = K
POISSON	mean = K
INTEGER	uniform on K to K
DISCRETE	values in C probabilities in C
UNIFORM	continuous on K to K
NORMAL	[mu = K [sigma = K]]
CHISQUARE	degrees of freedom = K
T	degrees of freedom = K
F	df numerator = K, df denominator = K

Minitab Commands

STORED COMMANDS AND LOOPS

The commands STORE and EXECUTE provide the capability for simple macros (stored command files) and loops.

STORE	[in 'FILENAME'] the following commands (*MINITAB commands follow*)
END	of the stored commands
EXECUTE	commands [in 'FILENAME'] [K times]
ECHO	the commands that follow
NOECHO	the commands that follow

DBASE IV COMMANDS

The following commands are a summary of the basic commands used in a routine dBase IV program. If any additional information is needed on these commands, consult one of the following sources:

- dBase IV Help screen (F1)
- dBase IV manual

COMMANDS		
	@ row,col SAY expression GET variable	Displays expression on the screen or printer at the specified coordinates. The value of variable is displayed on the screen for editing.
	ACCEPT [Prompt] TO variable	Reads a character value and stores it in variable.
	APPEND	Generates a full-screen display for adding new records.
	APPEND FROM filename	Adds records from filename to the file in *use*.
	ASSIST	Returns to the Control Center from the dot prompt or the F2 function key.
	AVERAGE expression list	Computes averages of the specified expressions from selected records.
	BROWSE	Displays the contents of a database file one screen at a time and enables the user to scan and make changes.
	CLEAR	Erases the screen.
	CLOSE DATABASES	Closes all open dBase IV files.
	CONTINUE	Resumes the search initiated by the last LOCATE command.
	COPY FILE oldfile TO newfile	Makes a duplicate of oldfile to newfile.
	COPY TO newfile	Copies selected fields and records from the file in *use* to newfile.
	COUNT	Counts selected groups of records.

CREATE filename	Creates a new file named filename (menu-driven).
CREATE REPORT rptname	Creates a custom report form (menu-driven).
DELETE	Marks specified groups of records as deleted.
DISPLAY	Display contents of specified groups of records.
DISPLAY STRUCTURE	Display structure details of the file in *use*.
DO CASE	Conditional branching structure with multiple paths.
DO filename	Execute the program stored in filename.
DO WHILE/ ENDDO	A program looping structure.
EDIT	Full-screen editing of selected groups of records.
EXIT	Causes immediate exit from a DO WHILE loop.
FIND string	Finds the first indexed record matching the specified character string.
GO BOTTOM	Go to the last record of the file in *use*.
GO TOP	Go to the first record of the file in *use*.
HELP	Calls up the dBase IV Help facility.
IF . . . ELSE . . . ENDIF	Conditional branching structure with two paths.
INDEX ON expression TO filename	Creates an index for the file in *use*.
INPUT [Prompt] TO variable	Reads a value and stores it in variable.
JOIN	Creates a new database file by bringing together designated fields and records from two OPEN database files.
LIST	Displays selected contents of a file.
LOCATE FOR condition	Finds the first record that satisfies the specified condition.
LOOP	Causes immediate return to the top of a DO WHILE loop.
MODIFY COMMAND filename	Creates a new program or edits an existing program.
MODIFY REPORT rname	Modifies the report form named rname (menu-driven).
MODIFY STRUCTURE	Changes the structure of the file in *use* (menu-driven).
PACK	Permanently removes all deleted records from the file that is currently open.

QUIT	Closes any open files, and exits dBase IV.
READ	Permits editing of any variables displayed by @ . . . GET commands.
RECALL	Removes the deleted flag from specified groups of records.
REPORT FORM rname	Generates a report of the file in *use*, using the named report form.
RETURN	Ends execution of a program.
SEEK expression	Finds the first indexed record matching the specified value.
SET BELL ON/OFF	Controls bell ringing during data entry.
SET DEBUG ON/OFF	Specifies output device for SET ECHO output.
SET DECIMAL TO n	Specifies the minimum number of decimal digits output in numerical operations.
SET DEFAULT TO n	Specifies the drive to be searched for various files.
SET ECHO ON/OFF	Specifies whether or not program commands are displayed at the terminal.
SET INDEX TO filename	Attach the named index to the file in *use*.
SET RELATION [TO expression] INTO alias	Establishes a relation between the file in *use* and another open file denoted by alias.
SET STEP ON/OFF	With STEP ON, a program pauses after each instruction execution.
SET TALK ON/OFF	With TALK ON, the results of various operations are echoed to the screen.
SKIP n	Reposition the pointer by n records.
SORT ON field list TO filename	Creates a sorted file ordered on the specified fields.
STORE expression TO variable	Stores the value of expression to the named variable.
SUM expression list	Computes sums of expressions from selected records.
TEXT/ENDTEXT	Defines boundaries of text to be output by a program.
TYPE filename	Outputs the contents of filename.
USE filename	Opens a valid dBase IV file.
WAIT [Prompt] [TO variable]	Interrupts program execution until a key is struck.

FUNCTIONS	CDOW (date-exp)	Day-of-the-week function; it returns the day in character form.
	CMONTH (date-exp)	Name-of-the-month function; it returns the month in character form.
	CTOD(exp)	Converts the value in exp to a date-type value.
	DATE( )	System date function; it returns the current date in character form.
	DAY(date-exp)	Numerical value of day of week (1–7).
	DTOC(date-exp)	The date-to-character function; it converts date value to a character string.
	EOF( )	The end-of-file function; it returns a value of true if pointer has moved past the last record.
	LEN(string)	Returns the length of string.
	MONTH (date-exp)	Numerical value of month (1–12).
	RECNO( )	The record-number function. Its value is equal to the record number of the current record.
	STR(num,b,d)	Converts num to a string b characters long, with d characters to the right of the decimal point.
	SUBSTR (string,s,b)	Returns a substring of length b from string starting at position s.
	TRIM(string)	Removes trailing blanks from string.
	UPPER(string)	Converts string to all uppercase.
	VAL(string)	Converts string to a numerical quantity.
	YEAR(date-exp)	Numerical value of year.

NAVIGATION KEYS	RIGHT ARROW	Move right one space or option.
	LEFT ARROW	Move left one space or option.
	DOWN ARROW	Move down one line, field, or option.
	UP ARROW	Move up one line or option. Move to previous field. Review or activate any of last twenty commands in history buffer (from dot prompt).
	PAGEDOWN	Display next screen or record. Move to first available option on current pull-down menu.
	PAGEUP	Display previous screen or record menu.
	END	Move to end of field. Move to last field in record. Move to last text/field on line. Move to last column of skeleton.
	HOME	Move to beginning of field.

	Move to beginning of record.
	Move to left margin.
	Move to first column of skeleton.
BACKSPACE	Delete previous character.
CTRL-BACKSPACE	Delete previous word.
TAB	Move to next field.
	Move to next tab stop.
	Move to next column.
SHIFT-TAB	Move to previous field.
	Move to previous tab stop.
	Move margin to previous stop.
	Move to previous column.
ENTER	Select currently highlighted option.
	Move to next field or line.
ESC	Abandon without saving changes.
	Return to previous menu or to Control Center.
	Cancel extended select.
DELETE	Delete currently selected item as character, field template, or block.
INSERT	Toggle Insert *on* or *off*.
CTRL-RIGHT ARROW	Move to beginning of next word or field.
CTRL-LEFT ARROW	Move to beginning of previous word or field.
CTRL-PAGEDOWN	Move to end of text.
	Move to current field in last record.
CTRL-PAGEUP	Move to beginning of text.
	Move to current field in first record.
CTRL-HOME	Move into a memo field.
CTRL-END	Save work and quit.
	Move out of memo field.
CTRL-ENTER	Save work.
CTRL-A	Move cursor to beginning of previous word.
CTRL-B	Move cursor to end of line.
CTRL-C	Move to bottom of screen.
CTRL-D	Move cursor one character to right.
CTRL-E	Move cursor up one line.
CTRL-F	Move cursor to beginning of next word.
CTRL-G	Delete one character at cursor.
CTRL-H	Act as backspace.
CTRL-I	Move to next tab.
CTRL-M	Add new blank line.

CTRL-N	Insert blank line between fields.
CTRL-Q	Abandon changes and exit.
CTRL-R	Move to top of screen.
CTRL-S	Move cursor one character to left.
CTRL-T	Remove word or field to right.
CTRL-U	Delete current field.
CTRL-V	Toggle Insert *off* and *on*.
CTRL-W	Save changes and exit the memo field.
CTRL-X	Move cursor down one line.
CTRL-Y	Delete all characters to right of cursor, including remainder of line.
CTRL-Z	Move cursor to beginning of line.

SUBJECT INDEX